Raging Forces

The 1991 eruption of Pinatubo, in the Philippines, left villages and farms frosted in an ashy volcanic haze.

Fire blazed over Iceland's fishing port of Heimaey when a 1973 eruption buried the town in coal-black cinders.

Raging Forces

LIFE ON A VIOLENT PLANET

GEORGE W. STONE

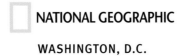

NATIONAL GEOGRAPHIC

WASHINGTON, D.C.

Hundreds of homes collapsed when a forceful 1992 temblor rattled Cairo, Egypt.

Contents

A tornado-like waterspout dances
with lightning in a deadly pas de deux
over Florida's Lake Okeechobee.

VIOLENT NATURE

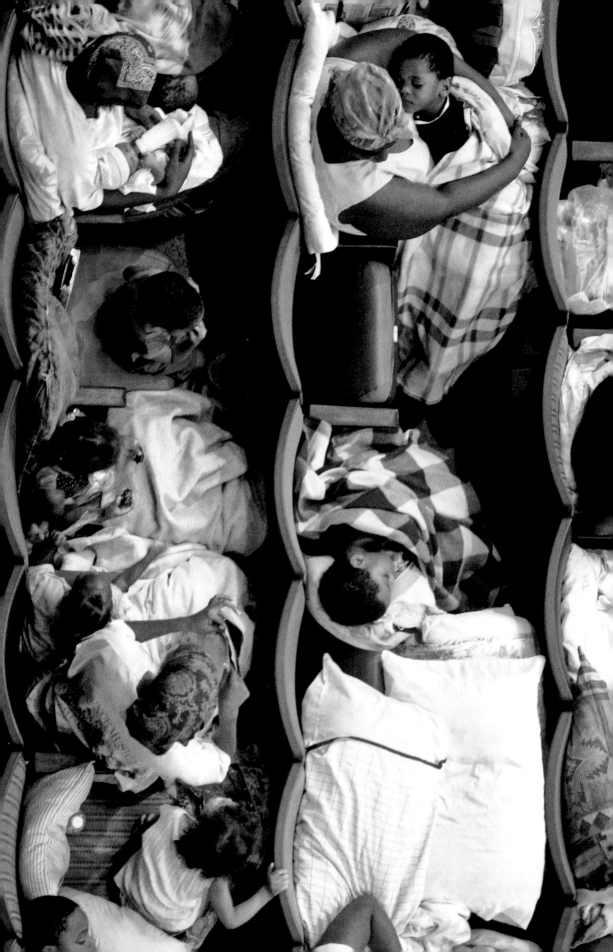

Violent Nature: What Are Raging Forces?

> "We can never have enough of Nature. We must be refreshed by the sight of inexhaustible vigor, vast and Titanic features, the sea-coast with its wrecks, the wilderness with its living and its decaying trees, the thunder-cloud, and the rain which lasts three weeks and produces freshets. We need to witness our own limits transgressed, and some life pasturing freely where we never wander."
>
> —HENRY DAVID THOREAU, *WALDEN*

Our planet is a perpetually evolving, chronically violent, ceaselessly churning, flame-singed, water-soaked, windswept, habitually inhospitable cosmic compound, wrapped around a molten iron heart, orbiting an atomic fireball. Our Earth home is by turns a life-sustaining sphere and a crucible of cataclysm, calamity, paroxysm, disease, disaster, and death. It always has been and always will be. "Civilization exists by geologic consent, subject to change without notice," historian Will Durant wrote famously. To geologic, one might add climatic, microbial, and individual consent, for the heavens above us, the cells within us, and the choices we make as Earth's most powerful inhabitants together prevail to help advance or defeat our civilization.

And yet, as Thoreau reminds us, we can never have enough of nature. At times we may have too much violent nature, which erodes the foundations of our civilized nature and places in jeopardy our very existence. But without the external and sustaining force of nature—the sun that heats us and asks nothing in return, the vegetation that feeds us, yet needs not to be fed by us—humanity would surely collapse not just into quiet desperation but into certain extinction. Should this happen, the world would not blink. "The planet we live on has merely to shrug to take some fraction of a million people to their death," writes pioneering environmentalist James J. Lovelock. "But this is nothing compared with what may soon happen; we are now so abusing the Earth that it may rise and move back to the hot state it was in 55 million years ago, and if it does, most of us, and our descendants, will die. It is as if we were committed to live through

Hurricane Katrina survivors in August 2005 shelter in New Orleans' sweltering Superdome.

The Fearefull Summer:

O R,

Londons Calamitie, The Countries Difcour-
teſie, And both their Miſerie.

Printed by Authoritie in *Oxford*, in the laſt great Infection of the
Plague, 1625. And now reprinted with ſome Editions,
concerning this preſent yeere, 1636.

With ſome mention of the grievous and afflicted eſtate of the famous Towne
of *New-Caſtle* upon Tine, with ſome other viſited Townes
of this Kingdome.

By IOHN TAYLOR.

A plague washed over London in 1625 with a deadly strain of
bubonic bacterium that claimed 40,000 lives.

the mythical tale of Wagner's *Der Ring des Nibelungen* and see our Valhalla melt in torrid heat."

Metaphors, such as Lovelock's, are among the tools we use to grasp at the enormity of the Earth's forces. They are especially valuable when describing natural disasters, events that are the consequence of the combination of a natural hazard, such as an earthquake or volcanic eruption, and human vulnerability. History's worst catastrophes have devastated humanity on a scale that is nearly unimaginable in its vastness. And they are difficult to envision because their grotesque scale bears almost no relationship to our own past experience. How does one, for example, conceive of a force so unfathomable that it kills roughly 230,000 people across an area from Indonesia to the east coast of Africa—within a single day? That's what happened on December 26, 2004, when a violent undersea earthquake pushed the Indian Ocean up into tsunamis that engulfed land and lives. How does one describe such a horror without trivializing it by cliché? How does one capture the cascade of catastrophe whose greatest impact, like the Black Death of 1347 to 1352 that killed 25 million people in Europe, is measured not in terms of scientific analysis but in terms of human lives lost? Millions upon millions of human fatalities. In an age where a single death is a tragedy, how can one begin to picture a time when 25 million tragedies were piled atop each other within five deadly years?

The simple formulation "disasters occur when hazards meet vulnerability" is a clinical definition of the impact of Earth's raging forces. It also suggests the inverse: When disaster strikes uninhabited areas with no human vulnerability, they cease to be disasters and become merely forces of nature. This book walks the jagged line between raw forces of nature and the peril they frequently impose on people. This book also enquires of the destructive impact humans have imposed on the original environment of their planetary home. *Raging Forces* visits many of the violent episodes that formed our planet and investigates the human attempts to comprehend these powers of nature through folklore, myth, religion, and science across the ages. History's catalog of cataclysm, from asteroid impacts to today's droughts, from Pompeii to Katrina and beyond, is more than a litany of destruction and waste. It is an anthology of events that, taken together, compose an integrated story of a living planet, of which we are but a small part. The capacity of humanity to survive disasters may be our greatest asset, just as the chance to understand these disasters—perchance to prepare for future events—remains our greatest opportunity.

NO ORDINARY DISASTER

Global catastrophe is often depicted in religion and myth as deserved punishment meted out by an exacting, all-powerul deity for the folly or wickedness of humankind. Ancient Greeks did not blame Atlas, who carried the planet on his shoulders, for earthquakes, but rather Poseidon, god of the sea, who rattled the Mediterranean and churned up tsunamis. With a few monstrous wing flaps, Hung Kong, the birdlike god of wind once worshipped in Taiwan, could create calamitous typhoons that swept the China Sea. Mongolian lamas conjectured that a giant frog carried the Earth on its back, delivering earthquakes with every troubling twitch. In Japanese mythology, the wind demon Fujin dashed across the heavens transporting breezes and typhoons in a bloated satchel that was prone to leaking. The Japanese god Raijin created thunder by beating on his ring of drums, while Namazu, a giant and restless catfish that lives in the mud beneath the earth, caused quakes in fishy fits of aggression. In Norse mythology, Thor's chariot brought thunder as it raced across the sky, and lightning bolts came from his mighty hammer strikes at the giants who constantly tormented him.

The mythological preoccupation with cosmic disaster is an appropriate bookend to its opposite conundrum, the riddle of creation, but it usually lends itself to more vivid imagery. Floods, in particular, are preferred tools of destruction. Fire, hurricanes, and pestilence are evergreens in the mythology of doom. "The greatest emphasis on global catastrophe is probably to be found in Mesoamerica," writes Roy Willis, a scholar of mythology. Aztec tradition held that a continuing conflict between deities led to cataclysms that engulfed four previous worlds. "The first era ended with the world being consumed by jaguars, the second was destroyed by a great hurricane, the third by fire and the fourth by flood. We are now in the fifth world, which is destined to be devastated by earthquakes," writes Willis. The Hopi people of Arizona held a similar version of

"A knowledge of the existence of something we cannot penetrate, our perceptions of the profoundest reason and the most radiant beauty, which only in their most primitive forms are accessible to our minds—it is this knowledge and this emotion that constitute true religiosity; in this sense, and this alone, I am a deeply religious man."

—ALBERT EINSTEIN, *THE WORLD AS I SEE IT*

this myth, with world-wrecking calamities ranging from fire to ice cover, flood, and a yet-to-be-revealed fourth apocalypse. Myths of natural calamities that collapse civilizations are stitched through history across cultures and traditions. Mesopotamian, Egyptian, African, Greek, Celtic European, Indian, Chinese, Malayan, Japanese, Australian, and North and South American mythologies all contain catastrophic imagery, some of which is life ending—and some of which sows the seeds for an improved state of affairs on Earth.

Biblical tales of disaster range from the monolithic—the flood that God sent to cleanse the world of its sinfulness, faithfully weathered by Noah on his great ark—to the multifaceted, such as the earthquakes, plagues, pestilences, hailstorms, thunderclaps, lightning strikes, burning mountains, and even a lake of fire, as threatened in the Book of Revelation. The mystery of such destruction beyond measure has sustained both fear and curiosity for thousands of years. In some cataclysms—such as the eruption of Mount Vesuvius that destroyed both Pompeii and Herculaneum in A.D. 79—nearly total annihilation left in its wake a peculiar immortality. Certain places on Earth are better remembered for the disasters they endured than for the unique accomplishments of their cultures. Such is the case with a pantheon of monomial calamities known the world over: Krakatau, Galveston, Johnstown, Pelée, Yungay, Tangshan, Heimaey, Kobe, Bam, Banda Aceh. The list, tragically, is endless.

But cataclysm can also be generative, as described in an Egyptian myth that depicts a primordial act of creation in the raising of a spot of land from the watery abyss that submerged the world. Tales from North America's Cheyenne people tell of a bird that salvages a beakful of mud from the boundless sea, which the All Spirit transformed into dry land. Charles Darwin, on his five-year global circumnavigation aboard the H.M.S. *Beagle,* collected observations—famously, on the Galápagos Archipelago in 1835. They enabled him to note similarities and differences in flora and fauna that fueled his theory of evolution by natural selection, published in 1859. From this event flow two observations. The first concerns upheaval. Fifteen active volcanoes now rise over the vaporous, humplike Galápagos Islands, which constitute a "hot spot" on the Nazca oceanic plate, 600 miles off the coast of Ecuador, encircled by cold water from the Antarctic. "Nothing could be less inviting than the first appearance," reported Darwin. "A broken field of black basaltic lava, thrown into the most rugged waves, and crossed by great fissures, is everywhere covered by stunted, sun-burnt brushwood, which show little signs of life."

However desolate, these remote, rocky sea discharges are today among Earth's most treasured and endangered places. Treasured for their enduring role as a wild and singular biosphere; endangered by a civilized world quickly encroaching on them. The fiery volcanism that disgorged these brittle spots of

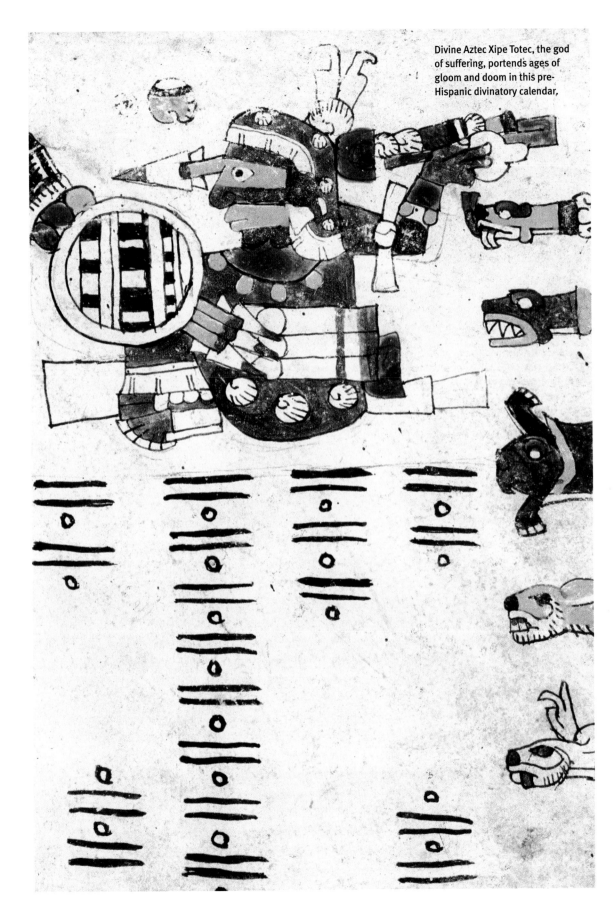

Divine Aztec Xipe Totec, the god of suffering, portends ages of gloom and doom in this pre-Hispanic divinatory calendar.

The Great Deluge: Floods Across Time

A limitless expanse of water is among the most common images of creation in world mythology. "Like the Hebrews, Babylonians, Greeks, Norsemen, and other peoples of the Old World, many Indian tribes of North and South America had traditions of the Deluge," wrote scholar Ella E. Clark, a collector of tribal tales. She recounts one myth, passed down by native tribes of Oregon, that describes the creation of Mount Jefferson peak following a series of three great floods. By the third flood—"bigger and deeper than any before [that] swallowed all the land and the people"—the people were ready with a massive cedar canoe that carried a chosen few safely to the foot of the mountain, where they repopulated their world. Although this myth alludes to the alluvial forces that shape the surface of our planet, it does not point to any specific historic event.

Other flood myths, especially from areas such as Egypt and the Middle East that are prone to random flooding along the Nile, Tigris, or Euphrates Rivers, can be traced hypothetically to actual events in history. In Sumerian myth, Ziusudra, king of Shuruppak, by building a boat survived a seven-day flood brought about by the gods to destroy humankind. This story is echoed in the epics of Atrahasis and Gilgamesh, and it likely influenced the Hebraic tale of Noah and the ark. Modern-day excavations in Iraq have shown evidence of a flood at Shuruppak that occurred in roughly 2800 B.C. In Greek myth, Zeus sends a deluge to punish humanity. Deucalion, the son of Prometheus, builds an ark and survives with his wife to reestablish the human race. Some archaeologists speculate that a massive Mediterranean tsunami, caused by the Thíra volcanic eruption on the Greek island of Santorini (in about 1630 B.C.), was the basis of the Deucalion myth. The Israelite crossing of the Red Sea has been linked by some historians to the identical tsunami, following the volcanic cataclysm at Thíra. Deluge myths span the globe. The legendary sunken kingdom of Cantref Gwaelod, off the coast of Wales, was a walled country protected from the sea by a dyke and ruled by Gwyddno Garanhir. When a drunken prince named Seithenyn neglected to guard the floodgates—left open by a fair maiden named Mererid—the sea swept through, inundating this "Welsh Atlantis."

One controversial explanation for the preponderance of flood imagery in myth is the Ryan-Pitman theory, which proposes that a deluge of catastrophic proportions surged from the Mediterranean Sea into the Black Sea in about 5600 B.C. This Black Sea deluge theory, which has been supported by evidence collected in recent archaeological expeditions, has been suggested as a possible source of Noah's flood, even though it challenges the dating of that legendary event. The event has also been connected to Plato's Atlantis myth and folk stories detailing the huge rise in sea levels that accompanied the end of the last ice age, some 10,000 years ago. Bruce Masse, an environmental archaeologist at the Los Alamos National Laboratory in New Mexico, has analyzed 175 flood myths from around the world and attempted to relate them

Fierce storms swept through southern China in June 2006, portending a reprise of past floods
that have historically haunted this nation.

to known, accurately dated natural events such as solar eclipses, volcanic eruptions, and asteroid
impacts. Half the myths Masse researched refer to a torrential downpour, and a third describe a
tsunami. Fourteen flood myths specifically mention a full solar eclipse, which Masse speculates is
a known event that occurred on May 10, 2807 B.C. Further research might someday conclusively
match many of the floods of mythology with the devastating deluges of geological history.

Whether an actual deluge once enveloped the world, or whether these waterlogged images
spring from the fertile mind of history's great mythmakers will never be known definitively.
Surely ancient cultures were as prone to exaggeration as modern ones, and although disasters
come in all sizes, they strike each individual in a personal, world-wrecking way. The process of
creating a story or constructing a myth around a natural disaster affords those affected by the
cataclysm some measure of control over the very forces that threaten to destroy life. In this sense,
there is valuable truth wrapped within the
fictions of myth. A global flood may seem
unlikely. But then along comes an event like
Hurricane Katrina to refresh our memories of
Earth's furious watery forces, and we realize that
storytelling is essential to survival.

"The face of places, and their forms decay;
And that is solid earth, that once was sea;
Seas, in their turn, retreating from the shore,
Make solid land, what ocean was before."

—OVID, METAMORPHOSES, XV

land between five million years and eight million years ago—in events not unlike those told in ancient myths of creation—enabled endemic species such as finches, boobies, mockingbirds, marine iguanas, and giant tortoises to gain purchase and forge distinct evolutionary paths. From this crucible of creation, we are reminded that it is not brute strength or fitness but adaptation, by luck or design, that offers the chance of survival. "Almost from the moment of its creation, a volcanic island is foredoomed to destruction. It has in itself the seeds of its own dissolution," writes Rachel Carson. In the Galápagos, however, one might add seeds of regeneration, for as the smoking fumaroles atop these precious crags prove, Darwin's young islands are still in the process of formation.

The second observation concerns time. More than 20 years passed between Darwin's journey and his publication of *The Origin of Species*. As his predecessor, Sir Charles Lyell, had observed in his own *Principles of Geology*, change on Earth had not happened as revolutions—periodic events so cataclysmic that they

Major Natural Disasters (From 1900-2005)

Earthquakes

Country	Year	Death Toll (est.)
China	1976	242,000
China	1927	200,000
China	1920	180,000
Indonesia/Sri Lanka/Thailand	2004	150,000
Japan	1923	143,000

Floods

Country	Year	Death Toll (est.)
China	1931	3.7 million
China	1959	2 million
China	1939	500,000
China	1935	142,000
China	1911	100,000

Droughts

Country	Year	Death Toll (est.)
China	1928	3 million
India	1942	1.5 million
India	1900	1.25 million
Former Soviet Union	1921	1.2 million
China	1920	500,000

Source: *Almanac of Geography*, National Geographic Society, 2005

Marine iguanas monitor the shores of the Galápagos Archipelago. The wrecked oil tanker in the background ran aground in 2001, spilling 170,000 gallons of diesel fuel.

could drive a species to extinction—but gradually, imperceptibly, over very long periods of time, through the action of constant forces such as wind and water. Lyell and other "uniformitarianists" believed that the Earth was old, change was slow, erosion was constant, and the whole process was continual. The decades it took Darwin to hone his theory on how a few particular species came into being—methodically testing and retesting his hypotheses at a pace that would cause apoplexy among today's computer chip-equipped scientists—constitute merely the faintest blink in geological time. And in the time since Darwin published his revolutionary, evolutionary theory, the Galápagos Archipelago has become one of the world's most coveted destinations for tourists and a desirable economic engine for residents—with both groups constituting an increasing threat to the very ecosystem they recognize as rare and endangered. "Darwin did not change the islands, but only people's opinion of them. That was how important mere opinion used to be back in the era of great big brains," wrote Kurt Vonnegut in his myth on reverse evolution, *Galápagos.*

Myth, however colorful and encoded, merely points to knowledge. By observing the actual forces of upheaval, placed within the fixed scale of time, Darwin was able to form a study of natural history that helped unlock one of the mysteries of biology—how random variations can form a competitive advantage that enables a species to survive. "When one man has reduced a fact of the imagination to be a fact to his understanding, I foresee that all men will at length establish their lives on that basis," wrote Thoreau. Thanks to the contributions of scientists such as Darwin, who have coaxed facts and understanding from myth, we as a civilization are better equipped to survive the raging forces that threaten to consume us. There can be no more valuable legacy than to have rescued life from the clutches of catastrophe. This gift is, in a broad sense, the protective value of myth and one practical end of science.

UPHEAVAL AND TIME

Climate, as well as geology, is a fundamental driver of human history. Its atmospheric element, weather, offers up this perpetual conundrum: that the only predictable aspect of weather is the near impossibility of predicting it. Make the wrong choice about carrying an umbrella, and you could end up drenched. Fly a kite into a lightning storm, and your fate could be much worse. But climate—the average state of weather over a period of weeks, months, and years—is among the ultimate raging forces that determine the fate of humankind. "Foule weather, lyeth not in a shower or two of rain; but in an inclination thereto of many dayes together," wrote Thomas Hobbes in *The Leviathan*. The violent inclination of the heavens, as we become increasingly aware, is not just a remote

and all-powerful force, but one that can be influenced by the actions of humanity, as well.

"How did anyone live in the Sahara?" asks anthropologist Brian Fagan in *The Long Summer: How Climate Changed Civilization.* "This world of sand and rock, of weathered outcrops and dunes, pressed on a completely different universe. The Nile Valley, a land so fertile that it nurtured the longest lived of all human civilizations, cuts across the desert from tropical Africa to the Mediterranean. For thousands of years, these two absolutely different worlds flourished alongside one another. Their different fates demonstrate the vulnerability inherent in any human response to climatic stress." Fagan has studied climatic changes and their effect on human civilization since the end of the last ice age some 10,000 years ago. The emergence of civilization and recorded history occurred in this Holocene period, as glaciers receded and global temperatures and sea levels rose. In this time, however, the climate has not produced endless abundance. Changing rain patterns have led to prolonged droughts that have brought down empires. Mini ice ages have crippled regions with lasting impact. Climatic upheavals have fueled epidemics and population migrations that blended societies to both tragic and

"I returned, and saw under the sun, that the race is not to the swift, nor the battle to the strong, neither yet bread to the wise, nor yet riches to men of understanding, nor yet favor to men of skill; but time and chance happeneth to them all."

—ECCLESIASTES 9:11

Hurricane Rita raged over the Gulf Coast in 2006, leaving a stream of gasoline and salt water in its wake.

Atlantis, a Submerged Utopia

Among history's most enduring mysteries is the legend of Atlantis, that "great and wonderful empire . . . beyond the pillars of Hercules" first mentioned by Plato in *Timaeus*, written about 360 B.C. According to the Greek philosopher, Atlantis was destroyed by earthquakes and floods within a 24-hour span, 9,000 years before his time. The questions that linger long after Plato's postulation tickle scholars' imaginations even today. Was there an Atlantis? If so, where was this utopia located, and what forces destroyed it? As explanations for Plato's inspiration, historians offer the theoretical Black Sea deluge of 5600 B.C., the Thíra eruption of 1630 B.C., the Trojan War, the deadly flooding and sinking of Helice in 373 B.C., or the failed Athenian invasion of Sicily in 415-413 B.C. Other scholars, both ancient and modern, view Plato's suggestion of a lost empire to be a metaphor for the ravages nature can wreak on humankind or for the catastrophes that can befall ideal states through unwise government.

In the centuries since Plato's claim, dozens of Atlantologists have "discovered" the lost city not just in the Mediterranean but all around the world, from Portugal and Ireland to Antarctica, Indonesia, and the Caribbean. Today few scholars hold out hope that this sunken utopia will ever be found, and yet even this skepticism is old news. Aristotle, for one, never believed in Plato's Atlantis. "Its inventor caused it to disappear," he is alleged to have uttered, according to the ancient Greek geographer Strabo.

Many academics today view Plato's tale of Atlantis as an invitation to examine our ideas of government and power, as well as the corruption that time brings, and not as a speculation on actual history or even a flight of the imagination from our greatest philosopher.

Atlantis raises the question: mythological utopia or lost treasure?

beneficial ends. This extended period of global warming has only accelerated over the past 150 years, and the future threats of global warming—such as drought or flooding along coastal plains—could bring devastation unlike any disaster humankind has previously known.

Global warming—the general trend of increasing surface temperatures throughout the world—is stoked by human activity, such as the burning of fossil fuels, which increases the abundance of greenhouse gases and, in turn, traps more of the sun's heat within the Earth's atmosphere. The United States currently generates more than 30 percent of the world's greenhouse gases. As China, India, and Brazil further industrialize, the carbon dioxide levels could double in the next 65 years. The catastrophic potential of this threat is massive, as reported by the U.S. Environmental Protection Agency: "Rising global temperatures are expected to melt polar ice. Warmer temperatures at the poles will change traditional ocean currents, winds and rainfall patterns. Changing

A Countrywide Disaster Profile

Event	Country	Year	Death Toll
Flood	China	1931	3.7 million
Drought	China	1928	3 million
Epidemic	U.S.S.R.	1917	2.5 million
Wind Storm	Bangladesh	1970	300,000
Earthquake	China	1976	242,000
Wave/Surge	Indonesia	2004	165,708
Volcano	Martinique	1902	30,000
Extreme Temperature	Italy	2003	20,000
Wildfire	U.S.	1918	1,000

Disaster Data Sorted by Continent

Event	Continent	Years	No. of Events	Death Toll
Drought	Asia	1900-2006	133	9.66 million
Flood	Asia	1900-2007	1,286	6.77 million
Epidemic	Asia	1900-2007	300	6.53 million
Earthquake	Asia	1901-2007	545	1.47 million
Wind Storm	Asia	1900-2007	1,219	1.10 million
Wave/Surge	Asia	1901-2006	36	235,843
Volcano	Americas	1900-2006	70	67,841
Extreme Temperature	Asia	1936-2007	109	18,079
Wildfire	Americas	1911-2006	110	1,470

Source: EM-DAT: The OFDA/CRED International Disaster Database (www.em-dat.net), Université Catholique de Louvain, Brussels, Belgium

This Bronze Age skeleton may reveal if a sixth millennium B.C. Black Sea deluge was the actual source of Noah's flood.

regional climate could alter forests, crop yields, and fresh water supplies. It could also threaten human health, and harm birds, fish, and many types of ecosystems. Deserts may expand into existing rangelands. [There is] likely to be an overall trend toward increased precipitation and evaporation, more intense rainstorms, and drier soils."

A raging force, indeed. The phenomenon of global warming, especially its cataclysmic potential impacts, remains an impassioned topic of debate. But no serious scientist denies that human activities dangerously accelerate the world's long-term warming trend on a scale most people find so difficult to comprehend that it remains easier not to imagine it at all. "Global warming, along with the cutting and burning of forests and other critical habitats, is causing a loss of living species at a level comparable to the extinction event that wiped out the dinosaurs 65 million years ago. That event was believed to have been caused by a giant asteroid. This time it is not an asteroid colliding with the Earth and wreaking havoc; it is us," writes Al Gore in *An Inconvenient Truth*.

What might an extinction scenario resemble in today's terms?

"If there is a message to take away from a look back at past predictions of potential calamity, it is that the risks of erring on the side of caution tend to be fewer than the costs of dismissing predicted threats out of hand," writes Eugene Linden, author of *The Winds of Change: Climate, Weather, and the Destruction of Civilizations*. "Even decades of insistent warnings could not prepare Americans for the actual horrors that Hurricane Katrina unleashed in August 2005. Turbo-charged by complacency, folly, and incompetence, Katrina destroyed a great city, transforming New Orleans into a septic stew of floating bodies, roaming gangs, disease, and toxic slime. The storm launched a wave of refugees not seen in the United States since the Dust Bowl, and the damage inflicted on crucial energy and transport infrastructure sent ripples throughout the economy."

Volcanoes, earthquakes, tsunamis, hurricanes, blizzards, droughts, wildfires, floods, plagues, pests, climate change, and global warming. The list of Earth's raging forces is lengthy, and the historic calamities caused by the collision of external nature and the human condition is without end. But the future is not a lost cause, and the forces that bring change may well be within humanity's reach. Our best example of bravery in the face of catastrophe might be Rachel Carson—author of *Silent Spring*, which examined the detrimental effects of pesticides on the ecosystem—who galvanized the global environmental movement. She wrote: "Those who dwell . . . among the beauties and mysteries of the earth are never alone or weary of life. Those who contemplate the beauty of the earth find reserves of strength that will endure as long as life lasts. The more clearly we can focus our attention on the wonders and realities of the universe about us, the less taste we shall have for destruction." ■

A worker in El Salvador tries to
clear the road after a 2005
mudslide overturned two buses.

Hurricane Katrina's howling winds and torrential rains destroyed Mississippi State Highway 90 in 2005.

PERILOUS
PLANET

CHAPTER 2

Perilous Planet:
A World of Possibility

"It's the Black sea in a midnight gale.—It's the unnatural combat of the four primal elements.—It's a blasted heath.—It's a Hyperborean winter scene.—It's the breaking-up of the ice-bound stream of Time."

—HERMAN MELVILLE, *MOBY DICK*

Earth's raging forces, so terrifying in their apocalyptic scale and unyielding in their apparent march toward oblivion, make it known that the planet's destiny and humanity's destiny—however mutually entangled they seem—do not necessarily lead to shared ends. Scientist E. O. Wilson writes, "Nature is that part of the original environment and its life forms that remains after the human impact. Nature is all on planet Earth that has no need of us and can stand alone." Admittedly, this is a reductive response, given the heavy footprint humans have left on soil and climate. But Wilson's formulation reinforces two important aspects of our planet's state: First, that Earth existed long before humans arrived on the scene. And second, that in all likelihood, our sphere will continue to orbit long after humans bid their adieus. "All the world's a stage, And all the men and women merely players: They have their exits and their entrances," wrote Shakespeare. The Bard was not thinking of humanity's dustlike irrelevance to the epochal spin of the globe, but his verse does reinforce the temporal biosphere that humans have inherited, and that has sustained a vast diversity of life, including our own.

But Earth's glacial evolution from chaos to order—if one favors such terms—is an endless tale of torments, tempests, and near total annihilation, with devastation layered atop devastation like the sedimentary walls of the Grand Canyon or the nine hellish circles of Dante's *Inferno.* The oldest rocks exposed in Arizona's Grand Canyon, for example, date back roughly 1.8 billion years; the limestone, sandstone, and shale sediments atop that layer document the entire 291-million-year span of the Paleozoic era. These sedimentary chunks reveal not just geological clues, but

Rock in Sledge Island, Alaska, is no match for the powerful forces of plate tectonics.

biological treasures, in the form of marine invertebrate fossils (sponges, sea lilies, corals) that help explain the origins of life. The forces that produced order in the Grand Canyon seem to have produced chaos nearby, such as in sections of the San Andreas Fault, where huge tilts, folds, and crumpled rock layers turn linear sediment on its side, adding mystery to the history of Earth's geology. These two visible examples illustrate the elasticity and eventual disintegration of rock under the creative, cataclysmic forces above and below the planet's surface. And they are nothing new in the 4.6-billion-year history of our world and its solar system.

In the late 18th century, French astronomer Pierre-Simon Laplace proposed the solar nebular theory, which holds that the sun and the planets each coalesced from a rotating cloud of cooling gases and dust in one arm of the Milky Way galaxy. The sun and the individual planets gained mass as their gravitational pulls attracted space debris ranging in size from dust to asteroids. Over the next billion years, Earth's surface evolved from a thin basalt crust to include granitic continental masses on shifting plates above a still molten interior. Gases, the pall of ash, and rivers of molten rock freed by volcanic explosions provided the beginnings of the first atmosphere as vents began releasing carbon dioxide and steam from the Earth's interior—steam that eventually condensed into oceans that gave life to blue-green algae. These organisms took the carbon dioxide from the primitive atmosphere and used energy from sunlight to manufacture sugar and starches. This miracle of photosynthesis released oxygen that accumulated to create the atmosphere necessary for life today.

The magic of Earth's atmosphere, which is gossamer thin in relation to the planet's corpulence, is its ability to insulate the surface from temperature extremes and protect it from excess radiation. This narrow range—which contains nearly all atmospheric gases within 20 miles and all weather within 10 miles above Earth—is the life-sustaining miracle of our planet. "It was Alfred Russel Wallace, cofounder with Charles Darwin of the theory of evolution by natural selection, who came up with the phrase 'the Great Aerial Ocean' to describe the atmosphere," writes Tim Flannery in *The Weather Makers*. "It's a far better name, because it conjured in the mind's eye the currents, eddies, and layers that create the weather far above our heads, and that are all that stand between us and the vastness of space." In the 19th century, a romantic and democratic era of scientific questioning produced great strides in meteorological, geological, and biological theory. Among the most important discoveries was an appreciation of the atmosphere's role in the advancement of life on Earth—from the single-celled organisms of the Precambrian era, which ended roughly 540 million years ago, to the profusion of life and emergence of modern humans in the current Cenozoic era, which began 65 million years ago (although modern *Homo sapiens* did not appear until 120,000 years ago). "The great aerial ocean, indivisible and omnipresent, has so regulated

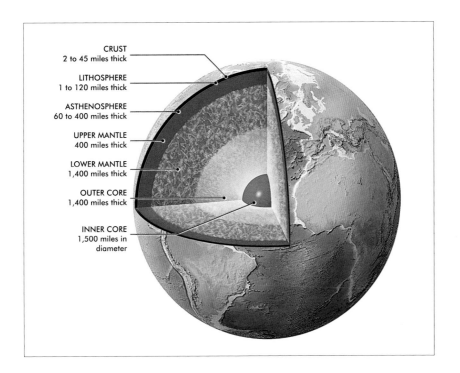

CRUST
2 to 45 miles thick

LITHOSPHERE
1 to 120 miles thick

ASTHENOSPHERE
60 to 400 miles thick

UPPER MANTLE
400 miles thick

LOWER MANTLE
1,400 miles thick

OUTER CORE
1,400 miles thick

INNER CORE
1,500 miles in
diameter

Travel to Hawaii Volcanoes National Park for abundant evidence of the volcanic fury that gave birth to this magnificent island chain. Such activity results when plates at the Earth's surface move over a source of molten material, eventually intersecting to dramatic effect.

A March 1966 blizzard in Jamestown, North Dakota, dumped enough snow to almost bury utility poles.

Planetary Extremes

136°F	Highest recorded temperature (Al 'Aziziyah, Libya, Sept. 13, 1922)
-129°F	Lowest recorded temperature (Vostok, Antarctica, July 21, 1983)
523.6 inches	Highest average annual rainfall (Lloro, Colombia)
0.03 inch	Lowest average annual rainfall (Arica, Chile)
75.8 inches	Maximum 24-hour snowfall (Silver Lake, Colorado, April 14-15, 1921)
231 mph	Strongest recorded gust of wind (Mount Washington, New Hampshire, April 12, 1934)

Sources: National Climatic Data Center/National Oceanic and Atmospheric Administration; National Climate Extremes Committee/NOAA

our planet's temperature that for nearly four billion years Earth has remained the sole known cradle of life amid an infinity of dead gases, rock, and dust. Such a feat is as improbable as the development of life itself; but the two cannot be separated, for the great aerial ocean is the cumulative effusion of everything that has ever breathed, grown, and decayed," says Flannery.

WINDOWS INTO THE WORLD

Millions of people are drawn each year to Wyoming's Yellowstone National Park, where a looking glass of natural wonders offers a glimpse into the ongoing energy of Earth's subterranean forces. Pools of Technicolor mud bubble, hiss, and pop. Geysers erupt through cracks and launch jets of hot water and vapor into the air. Billions of tiny bacteria create rainbows of flora in steaming lakes. The fiery heart of Grand Prismatic Spring, Yellowstone's largest hot spring, offers clues to Earth's molten nature. Brown, orange, and yellow algae ring the edges of this magma-heated pond, which steams at a sizzling 199°F. Yellowstone was formed as magma rose to within a few thousand feet of Earth's surface and forced a bulging, pressurized dome that cracked, creating channels for eruptive magma that exploded into the air. Millions of tons of ash covered thousands of square miles and darkened the sky over North America in an eruption that is believed to have been a thousand times more powerful than the 1980 eruption on Mount St. Helens, in Washington. The land surface covering the empty space under the ground following this eruption collapsed a mile downward, creating an ash-filled caldera 40 miles long and 30 miles wide, which geologists identified in the 1960s. But long before scientists identified this cataclysmic history, Yellowstone amazed and enchanted visitors who edged along hot-spring perimeters much like the namesake prismatic algae.

The Earth's metallic core—a ball of iron and nickel hotter than the sun but kept solid by the tremendous pressure around it—lies within a sphere of liquid metal that provides the planet's magnetic field. Atop this layer a slowly churning mantle of rock is kept in a plastic state, ranging in texture from liquid to clay, by heat and pressure. This molten mantle is topped by a cold, rigid crust of continents and seafloors that measures less than 50 miles deep. Mantle rock continuously rises toward the crust, cools, and sinks. This motion has cracked the thin crust into about 20 rocky slabs, or plates, which slowly drift on the mantle. Plates separate at rifts, where the plastic rock of the mantle, freed of overlying pressure, liquefies and wells toward the surface as magma; they collide at subduction zones, where the denser plate is forced down into the mantle. "Earth is living and dying, all the time creating and destroying its own

"Where from pure springs of unapproachable fire are vomited from the innermost depths; in the daytime the lava streams pour forth a lurid rush of smoke; but in the darkness a red rolling flame sweeps rocks with uproar to the wide deep sea."

—PINDAR, *PYTHIAN ODES*

Ethiopia's Dallol Depression, with mineral-rich pools and volcanoes, is the hottest place on Earth.

surface. It is a body in motion, alive—and in its vitality, awesome," observed Walter Cronkite in the foreword to *Exploring Our Living Planet* by Robert D. Ballard. His observation echoes that of Scotsman James Hutton, the father of modern geology, who proposed that our planet was in continuous but gradual change, constantly decaying and renewing itself. Hutton's theories, based on observations of geologic stratification, discredited widely accepted notions that the planet was 6,000 years old. He wrote in 1795 that the Earth had "no vestige of a beginning, no prospect of an end."

But this basic recognition of our ancient, malleable, and moveable planet took a long time to solidify. In the 15th century Leonardo da Vinci postulated

The Flare Up There

It's a whip of incinerating gases that explodes from the sun's 11,000°F surface with the force of millions of atomic bombs, stretches a distance equivalent to that from the Earth to the moon, and produces the solar system's most devious firecracker. A solar flare is a sudden burst of

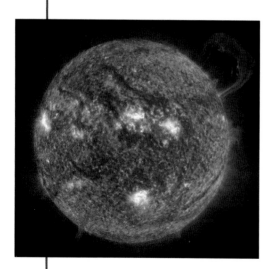

A wispy, hook-shaped prominence of dense plasma rises from the sun's hot, thin corona in this photograph captured by Extreme-ultraviolet Imaging Telescope.

electromagnetic radiation (radiation consisting of electric and magnetic waves and energy that travel at the speed of light) that erupts from the sun's surface and penetrates Earth's atmosphere with charged particles (plasma, electrons, protons, and other ions) that can knock out power grids, fry satellites, and disrupt radio transmissions. Although invisible to the human eye, this flare affair is the most intense outburst in the 11-year cycle of solar storms, and when its solar winds travel at about 600,000 miles per hour, they strike our planet with shock-wave fury. What else would you expect when the sun—a bundle of nuclear fusion with a core temperature of 27,000,000°F—sends us a telegram? A major flare in December 2006 prompted NASA to order the crews of orbiting space shuttle *Discovery* and the International Space Station to take precaution, while on Earth the electromagnetic storm generated magical northern lights, just in time for the holidays.

a rudimentary theory of crustal movement. As early as 1620 English philosopher Francis Bacon noted that the coastlines of western Africa and eastern South America seemed to fit together as puzzle pieces. About 150 years

"Wind feeds the fire, and wind extinguishes:
The flames are nourished by a gentle breeze,
Yet, if it stronger grows, they sink and die."
—OVID, REMEDIA AMORIS, I

later Benjamin Franklin proposed that our planet had a spherical core surrounded by fluids supporting its rocky shell. Building on the geological discoveries and fossil record findings of Hutton, William Smith, and Charles Lyell, German meteorologist Alfred Wegener in 1912 proposed a revolutionary theory: that the continents were once joined in a single landmass, which he called Pangaea (Greek for "whole earth"). According to Wegener's theory of continental drift, this super-continent began breaking up about 225 million years ago, first into two continents—Laurasia and Gondwana—which in turn cleaved into North America, Europe, and Asia, and later South America, Africa, Australia, and Antarctica. Today, North and South America continue to move away from Europe at a rate of 0.4 inch to 1.6 inches per year, while the Pacific Ocean shrinks, and India crashes into Asia at 2 inches annually. Geologists predict that in 150 million years Africa will have drifted north, squeezing the Mediterranean Sea into a channel, and the African and Eurasian continents will merge. If such movement still seems improbable, consider what naturalist John McPhee points out: "The summit of Mount Everest is marine limestone."

The idea of drifting, colliding, cleaving continents that float across the planet explains the origins of oceans and landforms, the continuity or isolation of flora and fauna, and the sources of powerful tremors and volcanic eruptions that wrack the Earth. Continental drift forms the foundation of plate tectonics, the geologic theory proposed in the 1950s and 1960s that slow-motion movement of thin, rocky layers that underlie continents and ocean basins is the raging force that defines our planet's physical features and capacity to support life. "All life exists in a thin layer embedded between two vast heat engines," explains geoscientist William Melson in *Forces of Change*. "One engine, which heats the Earth's oceans, atmosphere, and land, is driven by energy from the sun. The other engine is fueled by the Earth's internal heat, which results mainly from the slow decay of radioactive elements such as uranium and thorium." From either source heat builds unequally, creating convection currents in air, water, and even the rocks of the planet's mantle. The Earth's internal heat causes eruptions, earthquakes, rifts, and landslides, while solar energy sets up evaporation, winds, storms, droughts, and all other manifestations of weather.

VIOLENT BEAUTY

Out of rocks, fossils, and seismographs emerged a new conception of the Earth as shaped by raging forces over unfathomable spans of time. And yet not all change comes gradually. Meteor impact-driven mass extinctions have occurred periodically through our planet's history. The Permian Extinction, which may have been caused by a single comet collision, wiped out up to 96 percent of all ocean species and 70 percent of all land species. Fossil evidence indicates that the last of the dinosaurs disappeared some 70 million years ago in an environmental apocalypse brought on by events that are not clearly understood. One thing is sure, however—the land was rendered uninhabitable for up to 75 percent of plant and animal species. This event, which marked the end of the Mesozoic era (the age of reptiles) and the beginning of the Cenozoic era (the age of mammals), was the fifth in a line of great disturbances that scientists consider the history makers of life on Earth.

In 2006, scientists reported their discovery of an 18-mile-wide crater in the middle of the Indian Ocean, which they theorize was the site of a titanic asteroid or comet impact 4,800 years ago, which may have produced a tsunami at least 600 feet high—about 13 times as big as the 2004 Indonesian wave—and killed a quarter of the world's population. Although mainstream science has not validated their theory, if true this opens up the possibility that cataclysmic impacts may happen more frequently than every 500,000 to one million years, as is currently believed. A 20th-century event known as the Tunguska fireball of 1908 provided a visible reminder of the furious force planet-pummeling meteorites bring. With the force of 2,000 Hiroshima bombs, a massive stellar fireball exploded over remote Siberia with blinding light and deafening thunder observed 500 miles away. Trees in a 9-mile radius were incinerated, while some 60 million trees in a 25-mile radius were blasted to the ground. Reindeer were instantly turned to ash heaps. On the night of the impact, luminous clouds veiled northern Europe and ships could be seen far out at sea. Astronomers now speculate that Tunguska-like catastrophes occur every 300 years or so.

Cataclysmic threats to life come from within the Earth, as well. More than 14 million years before the eruption at Yellowstone, floods of basalt inundated the American Northwest, where volcanoes have historically erupted with enormous force and impact. Mount Mazama, for example, exploded about 4900 B.C., forming Oregon's Crater Lake. The largest volcanic event in the past two million years, the colossal Toba eruption on the Indonesian island of Sumatra some 70,000 years ago, is thought to have reduced global temperature for several years and reduced the global human population from one million to less than 10,000. Paleontologists speculate that this catastrophe accelerated the extinction of non-*Homo sapiens* and isolated small human populations that form the foundation of modern humanity. And the Thíra eruption in the Aegean Sea in about 1630 B.C. may have caused an unfathomable number of deaths from Crete to Egypt.

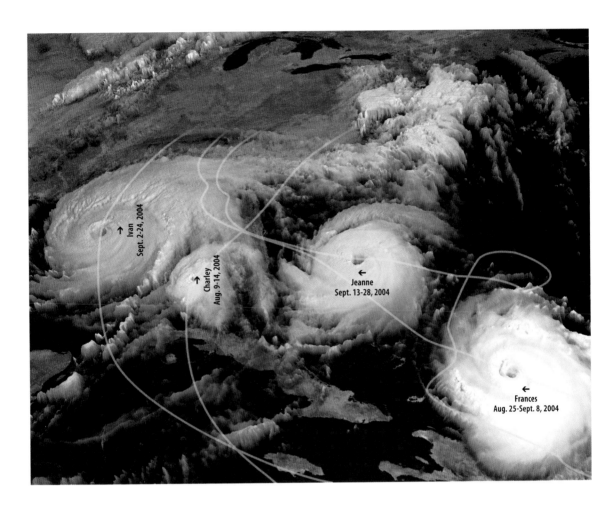

Ivan
Sept. 2-24, 2004

Charley
Aug. 9-14, 2004

Jeanne
Sept. 13-28, 2004

Frances
Aug. 25-Sept. 8, 2004

An onslaught of hurricanes slams into Florida and the Gulf Coast in this composite satellite image of storm tracks from August to September 2004, two of the most active months of Atlantic hurricanes on record. Once on the move, wind is steered by the Coriolis Effect, caused by the rotation of the Earth. The convergence and differing pressures of trade winds and midlatitude westerlies—blowing over heated tropical waters—can create the violent conditions for a perfect storm to form along the 30th parallel, at precisely the latitude of North America's Gulf Coast.

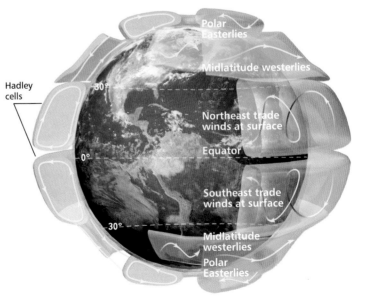

Polar Easterlies

Midlatitude westerlies

Hadley cells

30°

Northeast trade winds at surface

0°

Equator

Southeast trade winds at surface

30°

Midlatitude westerlies

Polar Easterlies

Heart of the World

"Virtually every ancient culture worldwide, and most religions, have shared a belief in some sort of mysterious subterranean world, inhabited by strange and powerful creatures, right beneath our feet," writes David Standish, author of *Hollow Earth*, which explores the curious history of imaginary worlds beneath our own. "The near-universality of these underworlds isn't surprising. They're the dark terrain of the unconscious given tangible form and structure, embodiments of the boogie-man who ran howling through our nightmares when we were kids."

The notion of a netherworld teeming with action and intrigue, crossed by rivers and mountains, spans civilizations and centuries, from the ancient Sumerians' Ki-gal to the Greco-Roman Hades, the Indian Naraka, Japanese Jigoku, Mayan Mitnal, Norse Svartalfheim, and Christian hell. (The "Middle-earth" of J. R. R. Tolkien's sagas was an ancient world from a fictional period 6,000 years ago, not a subterranean realm.) In the 17th century, hollow-Earth myths and religious beliefs began to carry a scientific mantle when English astronomer Edmond Halley presented his inner-Earth theory of independently turning concentric circles that had the ability to support life. Halley's scientific observations followed the work of German Jesuit Athanasius Kircher, whose writings and engravings present our planet with a fiery center—they are among the first attempts to define the science of inner Earth—and also mention underworld giants, dragons, and demons. Both theorists followed a long line of subterranean speculation depicted most famously, perhaps, in Dante's 14th-century epic journey through the gates of hell and into the nine circles of the *Inferno*.

In 1818 John Cleves Symmes rattled the scientific world with his announcement that "the earth is hollow and habitable within; containing a number of solid concentric spheres, one within the other, and that it is open at the poles." Although Symmes proposed an expedition, he never managed to explore one of his own theoretical holes; his idea, however, invigorated the hollow-Earth movement and sparked the imagination of writers such as Edgar Allan Poe and Jules Verne. Poe's *The Narrative of Arthur Gordon Pym of Nantucket* (1838) features a perilous voyage to the edge of the Arctic world and, perhaps though a Symmes hole, into speculative underworld territory. And Verne's *A Journey to the Center of the Earth* (1864) features an expedition down a volcano in Iceland into a realm of prehistoric animals, geological curiosities, and deadly hazards before the adventurers surface by riding an eruptive flow of lava that delivers them to the volcanic Italian island of Stromboli.

Subterranean realms soon became standard fare in science fiction, forming the settings of such titles as *The Goddess of Atvatabar, Tarzan at the Earth's Core, My Bride from Another World*, and *Upsidonia*. Although the hollow-Earth idea was widely ridiculed, some theorists went one step further: They rejected the notion that humans lived on the outside surface of a hollow planet and instead claimed that our universe itself lies in the interior of another world. Such is the power of human imagination—or the promise of a theory yet to be proved.

"The most striking sensation of a volcanic eruption is its limitless force," explains volcanologist Haraldur Sigurdsson. "That this is the biggest force on earth in terms of its amount of energy and material ejected. Eruptions give a sensation of awe, an exhilaration about the power of a volcano. It's almost like a religious experience in the sense that the earth has this huge power and it is capable of annihilation and total destruction. It's both thrilling and terrifying to realize that we don't know when the next big eruption will occur. All we know is that a supereruption will occur every 50,000 to 100,000 years, but prediction is improbable because geologists tend to monitor volcanoes that have erupted in the past, but the next supervolcano is unlikely to have erupted before." To give an idea of the scale of destruction a supereruption would bring, Sigurdsson begins with the ravages of past major events. "The 1980 Mount St. Helens eruption was relatively small in historical terms—Vesuvius ejected five times as much material. For an eruption of a different order of magnitude, we must go back to Tambora in 1815. This massive convulsion, the largest in recorded history, ejected ten times the amount of material as Krakatoa did. The eruption was so large that it killed 92,000 people. A tribe living on mountain slopes in North Tambora up the coast was exterminated and its language lost forever. Ash and other gases from Tambora created a pall that bounced back the

The algae-fringed Glory Pool provides a glimpse into the geothermal hot spot underlying Wyoming's Yellowstone National Park.

sun's rays, bringing global cooling—a 'year without summer'—and severe crop failure for at least three years. We have only an inkling of how such an event might affect today's technology-dependent society, but we do know it would cause significant global cooling. Ash floating in the jet stream and the stratosphere would make aviation impossible, and telecommunications would collapse because of interference with satellite and microwave transmissions. Pyroclastic flows and surges extending for thousands of miles would obliterate agriculture and destabilize regions."

The volcanic paroxysm of Krakatoa on August 27, 1883, is a modern version of the Vesuvius disaster that decimated Pompeii in A.D. 79. "The explosion itself was terrific, a monstrous thing that still attracts an endless procession of superlatives. It was the greatest detonation, the loudest sound, the most

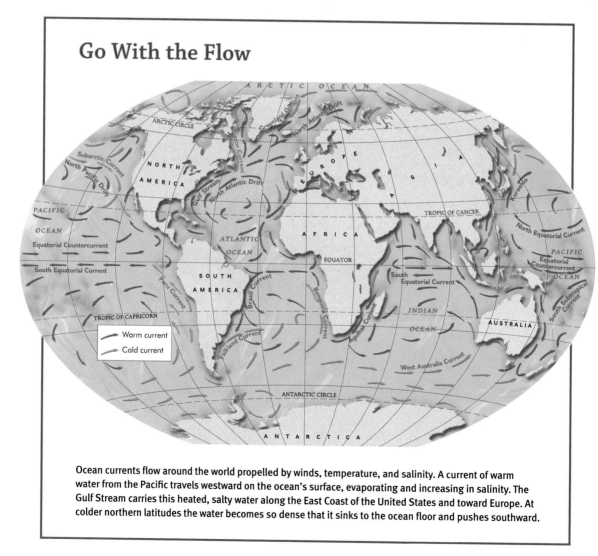

Go With the Flow

Ocean currents flow around the world propelled by winds, temperature, and salinity. A current of warm water from the Pacific travels westward on the ocean's surface, evaporating and increasing in salinity. The Gulf Stream carries this heated, salty water along the East Coast of the United States and toward Europe. At colder northern latitudes the water becomes so dense that it sinks to the ocean floor and pushes southward.

devastating volcanic event in modern recorded human history, and it killed more than 36,000 people," explains Simon Winchester, author of *Krakatoa: The Day the World Exploded,* a magnificent account of the eruption and the tsunamis that followed it. "The disaster left a trail of practical consequences—political, religious, social, economic, psychological, and scientific consequences among them. . . . In all sorts of other observable ways the impact of Krakatoa on the world's consciousness was profound. . . . Krakatoa had an impact on climate, for example: The airborne debris hurled into the skies lowered the planet's temperature; it changed the appearance of the entire world's sky; it set barometers and tide meters flailing wildly thousands of miles away; it panicked American firefighters into battling what they thought were raging infernos, but they were in truth violent sunsets caused by the roiling clouds of Krakatoan dust."

Volcanic eruptions cause death and destruction, and yet they are creative forces as well, with the power to unleash a violent beauty on Earth and within the atmosphere. *National Geographic* Editor Gilbert Grosvenor, reported on his 1924 expedition to Hawaii's Mauna Loa, majestically describing "a lumpy, rolling sheet of colored glass, extending as far as the eye could reach, glistening at times with the radiance of countless jewels, sparkling with the brilliance of diamonds and rubies and sapphires or softly glowing like black opals and iridescent pearls."

In detailing the magic of volcanic aerosols, the Krakatau committee of the Royal Society reported in 1888: "We saw green sun, and such green as we have never, either before or since, seen in the heavens. We saw smears and patches of something like verdigris green in the sky, and they changed to equally extreme blood red, or to coarse brick-dust reds, and in an instant passed to the color of tarnished copper or shining brass. . . . A glow comes up from the west like that of white-hot steel, reddening somewhat as it mounts to the zenith."

WINDS OF CHANGE

As far back as the fifth century B.C., the Greek philosopher Empedocles—perhaps with fuming Mount Etna in mind—interpreted volcanoes as creative rather than destructive forces. All things, according to Empedocles, can be reduced to four primary elements: earth, air, fire, and water. It is the coming together (*philia,* or "love") and parting (*neikos,* or "strife") of these elements that make up the asstonishing diversity of the physical world. Aristotle followed, ascribing quakes to exhalations from the planet's internal fire, which is stoked and empowered by heat from the sun and atmospheric breezes.

Indeed, the sun, sea, land, and atmosphere interact within a system of astonishing complexity. The sun unequally warms the Earth's surface, which then transfers heat and water vapor into the atmosphere, driving circulation and weather patterns as the planet attempts to bring temperatures into balance.

The inhospitable landscape of Antarctica—the coldest place on Earth—glows in blue and white.

With atomic fury the Tunguska fireball—most likely a comet or a stony meteorite that broke through Earth's atmosphere—exploded over the Siberian wilderness in 1908.

The wind acts as a great equalizer, forcing air to migrate as breezes or gales from high- to low-pressure zones. Winds are generated when warm air rises and expands, and cooler, denser air sinks and flows in to take its place. Once on the move, wind is steered by the Coriolis Effect, caused by the rotation of the Earth. At the Equator the planet spins at a speed of 1,041 miles per hour; this velocity decreases with increasing latitude and approaches zero at the Poles. In the Northern Hemisphere, this disparity deflects winds from west to east. The directions are reversed in the Southern Hemisphere, and winds blow from east to west. The Coriolis Effect helps divide each hemisphere into three wind belts: the trade winds, the midlatitude westerlies, and the polar easterlies. In both hemispheres small zones with surprising characteristics separate the wind belts. Near the Equator, where northeast and southwest trade winds meet, lies an area of calm known as the doldrums. The rising hot air of a Hadley cell, a convection loop of rising and descending air, causes these low-pressure troughs. The horse latitudes, a high-pressure zone where sailing ships delayed by lack of winds were sometimes forced to throw cargo horses overboard to conserve water, occur where trade winds meet the prevailing westerlies. Poet Samuel Taylor Coleridge sonorously described such windlessness in *The Rime of the Ancient Mariner:* "Day after day, day after day / We stuck, nor breath nor motion; / As idle as a painted ship / Upon a painted ocean."

Violent westerlies known as the roaring forties and furious fifties (named for their approximate latitude) made for suicidal sailing adventures around Cape Horn at the southern tip of South America and on the western coast of Australia. The polar front occurs where the cold polar easterlies meet the prevailing westerlies. The difference in pressure between these two winds can create dramatic weather in the polar zones, including 190-mile-per-hour katabatic winds (from the Greek, meaning "going downhill"), freezing and dry gales that rage over Antarctica, creating the most consistently windy place in the world. Complicating air circulation are mountains, lakes, and other surface variations that jumble and heap wind patterns.

When fickle winds fail to stick to predictable patterns freakish weather sometimes follows, threatening isolated catastrophes or dramatic climatic changes. A shift in the jet stream can cause a ripple effect that brings cold snaps, heat waves, droughts, or pounding rains, leading to floods, crop failures, and famine. The last millennium, for example, began on a warm note, with glaciers retreating and permitting Vikings to explore calm North Atlantic waters. But from the 14th century to 1850, the jet stream took a southerly spin, pushing cold polar air into Scandinavia, England, France, and even Italy, creating a catastrophic phenomenon known as the little ice age. Winters lengthened and growing seasons in Europe were shortened by a month, leading to widespread famine. In the 20th century, unusual circulation patterns in the summer of 1930 generated a deadly heat wave that marked the beginning of an extended drought that parched the United States from New York and Pennsylvania across the Great Plains to California. A "dust bowl" covered about 50 million acres in the south-central plains during the winter of 1935-36. Another devastating American heat wave blew superheated winds across the nation in 1995, peaking at 106°F in Chicago, where extreme weather and civic mismanagement led to a week of water shortages, power outages, hospitalizations, and 739 deaths. The summer of 2003 was one of the hottest ever in Europe, stoked by an incinerating August heat wave that left at least 35,000 and as many as 50,000 dead. France and Italy, which sweltered under sustained 100°F temperatures, experienced the majority of fatalities. The heat returned in July 2006, when a hot-air furnace blasted across the United States and over Europe.

Earth's global wind system is the driving mechanism for surface ocean currents, which transport heat from the tropics to the polar regions, influence the location of major fisheries, and affect coastal climates and human settlement patterns around the world. Tides, the regular rise and fall of ocean levels caused by the gravitational pull of the sun and moon, are assemblages of waves, the temporary motion of the ocean caused by storms and regional winds. Currents are the ocean's climate-driver, governing water temperatures and directly affecting atmospheric humidity and precipitation. The Humboldt (or Peru) Current, for example, extends along the west coast of South America from northern Peru to the southern tip of Chile, generating upwelling—where nutrient-rich deep water rises to replace warmer surface water—that supports an extraordinary abundance of marine life, which in turn sustains human populations.

This vital marine ecosystem is named for Prussian naturalist Alexander von Humboldt, whose Latin American journey from 1799 to 1804 is celebrated as the second scientific discovery of South America. Humboldt's lifelong quest to discover the unity within nature's great complexity left a meaningful and lasting impact on physical geography, meteorology, oceanography, botany, and biology. An early proponent of what became continental drift theory, Humboldt observed that New World volcanoes fell naturally into linear groups, presumably corresponding with vast subterranean fissures, thus anticipating the identification of the Pacific Ring of Fire and presaging plate tectonic theory. In South America, Humboldt mapped more than 1,700 miles of the Orinoco River, scaled the Andes, and discovered and measured the Peruvian current. As a botanist he was fascinated by the global distribution of organic life and its adaptive manifestations under the physical conditions of its biosphere—inspiring Charles Darwin (who called him "the greatest scientific traveler who ever lived") on his own voyage of discovery. To Humboldt, who is often credited as the founder of modern geography, creation and annihilation were born of the same raging force that also made it possible for life to succeed on Earth. His multi-volume work *Cosmos* was a collection of everything he knew about our world, including the interaction of humans and the natural events that shape our lives. "I am more and more convinced that our happiness or unhappiness depends more on the way we meet the events of life than on the nature of those events themselves."

Enriched beyond measure by the contributions of curious minds, like those of Bacon, Humboldt, Darwin, and Wegener, our understanding of Earth's raging forces has come a long way from the terrifying and confusing ages when natural catastrophe was seen as the work of an all-powerful deity—vengeful or merciful, depending on the result. As recent cataclysms such as the earthquake in Bam, Iran, on December 26, 2003; the Indian Ocean tsunami of December 26, 2004; and Hurricane Katrina, in August 2005, refresh our awareness of nature's awesome, catastrophic powers, the discoveries of history's great speculators offer some explanation for the causes of our planet's indiscriminate rampages and some hope for minimizing the consequences of these natural crises in the future. ■

A July 2006 flood in Ganzhou, China, following Typhoon Kaemi washes houses away.

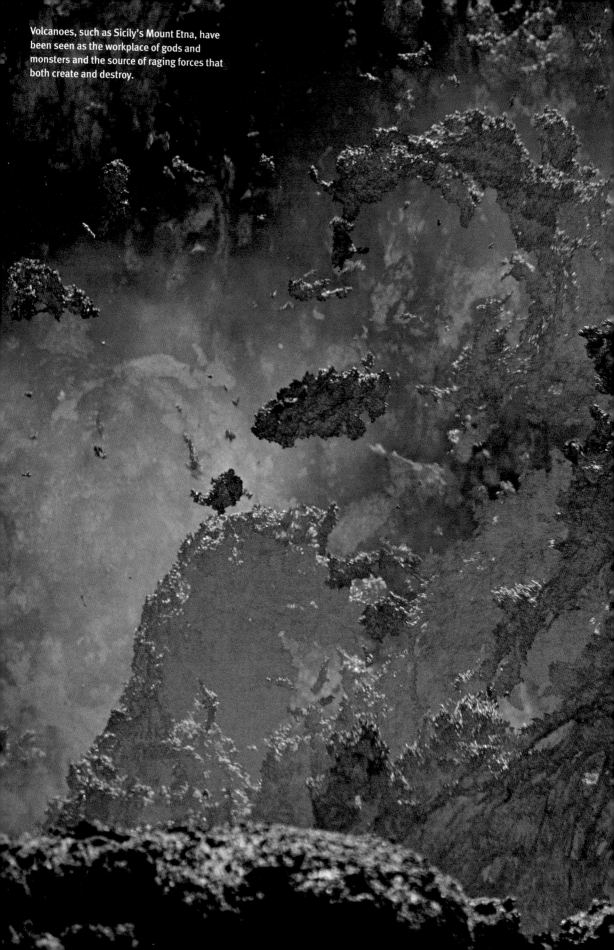

Volcanoes, such as Sicily's Mount Etna, have been seen as the workplace of gods and monsters and the source of raging forces that both create and destroy.

MOLTEN
EARTH

CHAPTER 3

Molten Earth:
Volcanoes and Fire-Breathers

"The sun turns black, earth sinks in the sea,
The hot stars down from heaven are whirled;
Fierce grows the steam and the life-feeding flame,
Till fire leaps high about heaven itself."

—*THE POETIC EDDA: VÖLUSPÁ*

The glacial face of Iceland covers one of the most active volcanic regions in the world. This island, a visible seam that straddles the Mid-Atlantic Ridge, is an eerie assemblage of volcanic landforms, geysers, ashy plains, smoky bays, glowing fissures, and fire-breathing mountains. Volcanic fury forms the fiery heartbeat of this North Atlantic nation, settled in the ninth century A.D. by Vikings who recorded and mythologized the terrestrial turbulence of their living landscape. Some settlers imagined rugged lava flows, volcanic vents, and jagged, impassable plains to be the sculpted remains of a timeless battlefield, where immortal gods had once waged a merciless war. Hekla, Iceland's most fervent volcano, has seen perhaps 30 cataclysmic eruptions since a devastating event in 1104; as a result, in medieval Icelandic folklore, Hekla was seen as an entrance to hell. Its crest swirled with vultures and ravens, its crannies served as gathering places for witches, and the wailing souls of the fallen could be heard around its base.

In 1963, the Vestmannaeyjar ("the islands of the men of the west") made international headlines when an underwater eruption forced to the surface a new island, later named Surtsey after Surtur, a Norse god of fire, who rules over Muspelheim, the lowest and most desolate region in Norse mythology. The literary *Völuspá,* part of the Icelandic *Poetic Edda* probably written sometime between A.D. 1000 AND A.D. 1300, describes the fire giant's dreadful, deadly power: "Surtur from the south, wielding fire / The gods' swords shine in the darkness, like stars in the night / Mountains collapse into rubble, And fiends shall fall." The Völuspá poem, which depicts Ragnarök—the fabled battle at the end of time—was written

Eldfell gushed fiery lava and ash over the Icelandic fishing port of Heimaey in a 1973 eruption.

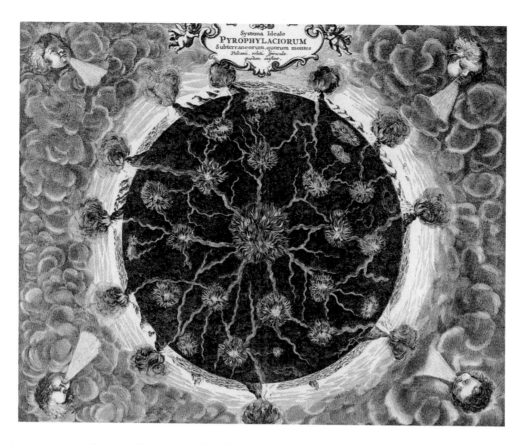

Seventeenth-century scholar Athanasius Kircher envisioned the world's furnace as a central fire, which fueled lateral fires and vented through volcanoes.

at the end of the heathen era and the beginning of the Christian age in Iceland. The text stands today as an invaluable source on Norse mythology and a fascinating window onto the creation and doom of the pre-Christian Nordic pantheon.

A decade after the surprising birth of Surtsey, inhabitants of the tiny town of Vestmannaeyjar on the island of Heimaey, a bit more than six miles south of Iceland, watched in terror as a massive eruption at Eldfell ("fire mountain") spewed ash and lava bombs on their small fishing port. On the morning of January 23, 1973, a thunderous fissure blasted a curtain of fire across the entire island. Boiling rivers of lava and hot ash engulfed a third of the town, and lava streams threatened to seal the harbor as the island's 5,300 residents were evacuated to the mainland. "At a distance of 50 miles, the inky horizon shimmered with an eerie red glow," reported Christopher Byron in *Time* in 1973. "At a distance of five miles, fly ash and stones peppered the plane's cockpit, making the sort of sound one hears when driving through a swarm of locusts. As we came still closer, fountains of flaming rock hurled up past us in the night, reaching heights twice that of the Empire State Building. The night turned from black to red, and the air smelled like sulfuric fumes from 100 billion burned-out kitchen matches. It was as if the twin-engine Piper aircraft were a mere gnat hovering at the open door of a blast furnace."

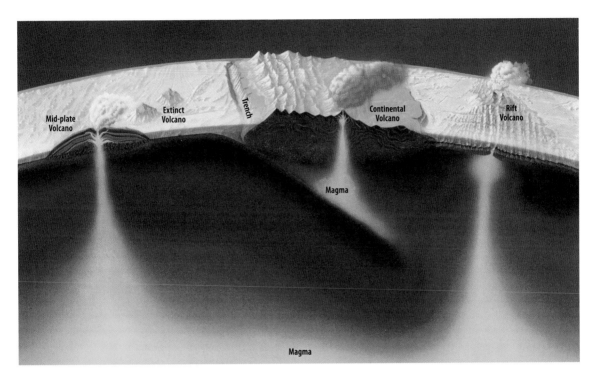

Three basic types of volcanoes erupt magma from the Earth's molten interior; each is born of the restless shifting of Earth's tectonic plates.

Eruptions blasted for two weeks as determined islanders mounted a bold defense against the mountain. Using hastily installed fire hoses and water pumps, the villagers sprayed the encroaching lava with water, later supplemented by seawater from a pump ship and pumps transported from other countries. The seawater—which was largely focused behind the lava flow—increased the lava's viscosity and thus slowed its rate of advance, and it was diverted away from town and into the sea. Miraculously, by the time the eruption's rage faded, the lava had formed a new spit of land that actually fortified the town's harbor. One death was reported.

What forces are behind the thundering, belching, sulfuric smoke and violent fire fountains that gush forth from the craggy crevices of the underworld? Well into the Middle Ages, many people thought of volcanoes, with their fiery summits and unearthly roarings, as the hellish world of suffering sinners. But as science evolved, so, too, did our understanding of the earth's fiery nature. This emergence of theories to explain out planet's rumblings is among history's most fascinating stories.

ANCIENT FIRE-BREATHERS

What causes volcanoes to erupt? How does Earth turn solid rock to flaming rivers? Throughout the ages, long before modern science offered answers to these questions, the ancients developed myths based on observations of the fiery phenomena of volcanic eruption. Some Greek writers accounted for the continuous rumblings and smoking in ancient times atop Sicily's Mount Etna by ascribing them to the noisy struggles of Typhon, the dragon Zeus had imprisoned under the volcano's bulk. One story has Hephaestus, the god of fire and metalcraft, exiled from heaven and working his forge on the Aegean island of Lemnos, pumping his bellows and lobbing hot rocks in the air. Roman tradition fostered the myths of Vulcan, the fire god, working his forge deep within a mountain on an island near Sicily, in a myth from which the word "volcano" is derived.

Mount Etna's name comes from the Greek *aitho,* for "I burn." The frequent explosions and lava flows of this nearly 11,000-foot-tall volcano—the highest

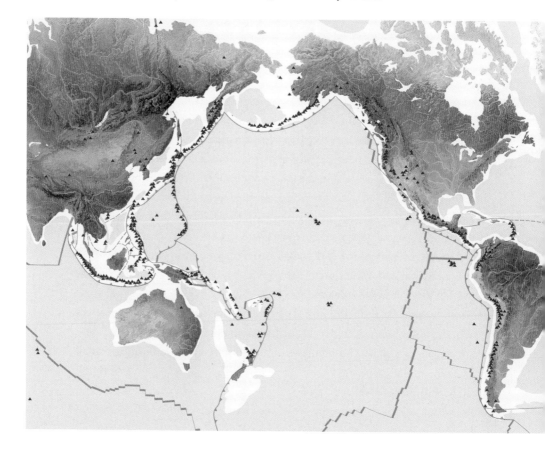

The global distribution of volcanoes above sea level is revealed by red dots, most of which mark the boundaries of Earth's tectonic plates. The Pacific Ring of Fire is visibly volcanic.

active volcano in Europe—have been recorded since 1500 B.C., and it continues to sputter, fume, and erupt today, making it Earth's most consistently active mountain of fire. The apparent rage of Etna has entranced poets and historians from antiquity. Plato sailed from Greece in 387 B.C. just to gaze at it. A vengeful Cyclops was said to hurl boulders at Odysseus from atop it. And, despite the fact that its eruptions rarely cause human fatalities, Etna has inspired observers to transcend myth as an explanation for volcanic activity and to begin forging solid theories that would, over time, form our modern understanding of eruption. One early scientific theory of eruption was posed by 17th-century Jesuit Athanasius Kircher, who studied eruptions at Etna and visited the crater at Vesuvius before publishing his vision of Earth, with a central fire connected to numerous others caused by the burning of sulfur, bitumen, and coal. His *Mundus*

Recently Active "Decade" Volcanoes

The International Association of Volcanology and Chemistry of the Earth's Interior keeps close watch over 16 Decade Volcanoes—seething cauldrons deemed worthy of study due to their history of large, destructive eruptions and proximity to populated areas.

Avachinsky-Koryaksky, Kamchatka, Russia

Colima, Mexico

Mount Etna, Italy

Galeras, Colombia

Mauna Loa, Hawaii, U.S.A.

Merapi, Indonesia

Nyiragongo, Democratic Republic of the Congo

Mount Rainier, Washington, U.S.A.

Sakurajima, Japan

Santa María/Santiaguito, Guatemala

Santorini, Greece

Taal, Philippines

Teide, Canary Islands, Spain

Ulawun, Papua New Guinea

Mount Unzen, Japan

Vesuvius, Italy

A fresh, sticky, silica-rich lava flow pours from a collapsed spatter cone at Tanzania's Ol Doinyo Lengai volcano.

Subterraneus (1665) is an 800-page miscellany of knowledge and speculation about the Earth's interior, including discourses on underworld giants, dragons, and demons, as well as his notion that the Earth has a fiery center, with hand-made etchings to illustrate this theory.

From the ancients to the moderns there's been "an evolution of ideas regarding volcanic activity," explains volcanologist Haraldur Sigurdsson. "Initially, volcanoes were viewed as manifestations of evil forces in the earth and their activities were related to activities of giants, gods, or spirits. . . . In Greece, the battle between the gods and giants, between positive and evil forces, is regarded by many people as an allegory for volcanic eruption. . . . The ancient Greeks were also the first to explain eruptions as an escape of winds from within the Earth. Later, the Romans hatched the idea that combustion was taking place within the Earth, causing other materials to melt and so unleash an eruption. That

Hyperactive Mount Etna bursts into molten lava, creating a violent jewel crowning the lights of Catania, Sicily.

theory held sway right through the seventeenth and eighteenth centuries, when scientists reached the more accurate view that Earth's interior is very hot and volcanic activity releases molten material through vents in the surface. But then nineteenth-century studies of tides reached the conclusion that our planet is essentially rigid, not molten inside. . . . The major revolution in understanding melting in the Earth and the origin of volcanic rocks did not emerge from geology but from the mid-nineteenth-century science of thermodynamics—the study of the fundamental laws of energy and heat," Sigurdsson says. "[N]o scientist could come up with a mechanism whereby rocks could move from a deeper to a shallower level with the Earth until the 1904 discovery that the radioactive decay of certain chemical elements provides the heat source to drive the convection currents. When we discovered in the 1960s that the planet is covered in moving plates, the theory of plate tectonics was solidified."

EXPLOSIVE DISCOVERY

A volcano is a landform that develops around a weakness in the Earth's crust from which molten magma, disrupted preexisting volcanic rock, and gasses are ejected or extruded. Volcanoes are not randomly distributed over the Earth's surface, but are concentrated on the edges of continents, along island chains, and beneath the sea, forming long mountain ranges. But before examining the different types of volcanoes and their eruptions, it's essential to investigate how magma erupts onto the surface of our planet and why more than three-fourths of the Earth's surface is of volcanic origin.

Over the course of geological eras, the surface of Earth has continuously shifted, creating new oceans and closing off others, pushing up towering mountain chains along the boundaries of continents, lifting ocean floors thousands of feet above sea level, creating new oceans and closing off others. The scientific explanation of such movements is the theory of plate tectonics. This revolutionary idea holds that our planet's outer skin is made up of about 12 large slabs (and several minor ones) called tectonic plates—from the Greek *tekton,* meaning "carpenter" or "builder." These plates may measure thousands of miles across, but with a depth of 50 miles or less are comparatively thin—about the same in relation to the Earth as an eggshell to an egg. Riding atop these crustal plates are continents. As the plates travel at the speed of an inch or two a year, they grind against one another, triggering eruptions and earthquakes along their margins. Such plate collisions can cause huge slabs of the Earth's crust to thrust downward, creating an ocean trench and allowing buoyant and lighter magma to rise through fractures toward the surface. As magma rises, the pressure on it drops, and water and such compounds as carbon dioxide and hydrogen sulfide form bubbles that can occupy as much as 90 percent of the volume of the rising magma. Explosive energy comes from the high-pressure gas and other volatile substances in the bubbles.

The reshaping that results from plate tectonics gives rise to volcanic chains, such as the Andes; causes mountain chains like the Himalaya and the Pacific Northwest's Cascade Range to uplift; and forms huge strike-slip land rips, like the San Andreas Fault. Not all mountain systems created by plate movement are visible. As plates move apart they create a second class of volcano exemplified by the Mid-Ocean Ridge, an underwater mountain range 46,000 miles long. Here seafloor spreading causes magma to be extruded continuously. The ocean floor near the ridge is 200 million years old or less, making it among the youngest material on Earth. The Mid-Atlantic Ridge actually reaches above sea level in such places as Iceland, which itself sits atop a third class of volcano: the hot spots. The Hawaiian Archipelago was formed when a region of hot, upwelling magma—a mantle plume—caused melting of the overlying plate, creating a hot spot, which sent magma skyward. And yet, despite new material being added to

Large-scale excavations of Pompeii in the late 19th century uncovered a lost world of treasure and tragedy. The ruins of Pompeii, destroyed in A.D. 79, were rediscovered in 1748. Thousands of victims suffocated from toxic gas inhalation and were subsequently buried in plumes of ash, which immortalized their moment of doom. Carefully poured plaster molds capture tragic poses of human suffering once encased in volcanic ejecta.

its surface, our planet is not growing in size; instead, Earth destroys as much crust as it creates, recycling old rock along boundaries where oceanic and continental plates converge.

Encircling the Pacific Ocean, tracing the seams where these giant plates collide, is a crescent of volcanoes known as the Pacific Ring of Fire. Sections of ten different tectonic plates collide around the edges of this 29,825-mile arc, creating a convergence zone where more than half of the world's active volcanoes above sea level are found and the majority of significant earthquakes occur. This fiery loop of more than a thousand volcanoes is a dynamic zone that has seen some of history's most deadly catastrophes, including the eruptions of Krakatau, Pinatubo,

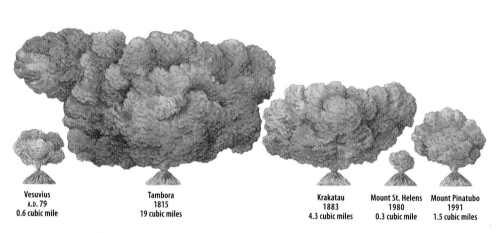

Vesuvius	Tambora	Krakatau	Mount St. Helens	Mount Pinatubo
A.D. 79	1815	1883	1980	1991
0.6 cubic mile	19 cubic miles	4.3 cubic miles	0.3 cubic mile	1.5 cubic miles

In terms of the relative volume of ejecta emitted, Tambora's 1815 eruption takes the prize.

History's Ten Deadliest Volcanoes

Volcano	Deaths	Year
Tambora, Indonesia	92,000	1815
Krakatau, Indonesia	36,417	1883
Mount Pelée, Martinique	29,025	1902
Ruiz, Colombia	25,000	1985
Unzen, Japan	14,300	1792
Kaki, Iceland	9,350	1783
Kelut, Indonesia	5,110	1919
Galunggung, Indonesia	4,011	1882
Vesuvius, Italy	3,500	1631
Vesuvius, Italy	3,360	79

Source: Gates, Alexander E. and David Ritchie, *Encyclopedia of Earthquakes and Volcanoes*, 3rd ed. Facts on File, 2007

Fuji, and Mount St. Helens. The world's largest concentration of active and dormant volcanoes lies along the Pacific Ring of Fire. Throughout history, this seismic zone has produced both volcanic eruptions and earthquakes to earth-shattering effect. But since the majority of the volcanic cones within the Pacific Ring of Fire peak far beneath the ocean's surface, this zone doesn't always reveal its fiery nature.

But these submerged, ocean-ridge cones represent just one of the basic types of volcano produced by the specific geodynamic conditions of its location. From tiny heaps of cinder to towering cones whose snowy summits pierce the clouds, volcanoes vary tremendously in shape, size, and eruptive behavior. They also change shape during their lifetimes. A volcano's form is generally determined by the kind of eruption—explosive or effusive—it produces, and this is largely dependent on the chemical composition of the lava it erupts. The chemical and mineralogical constituents of nearly all kinds of lava are virtually identical—silica and oxides of calcium, sodium, aluminum, potassium, sulfur, magnesium, and iron—but they vary considerably in their proportion. There are ten general types of volcanic structure—stratovolcano, compound volcano, shield, caldera, soma, fissure, lava dome, cinder cone, tuff cone, and table mountain—and the prevalent activity ranges from explosions and effusions to hydrothermal activity (fumaroles, hot springs, geysers) and related phenomena such as lahars (avalanches of mud and debris), tsunamis, and gas clouds.

Volcanic mountains built almost exclusively of thin, low-silica lava flows are called shield volcanoes, so named for their supposed resemblance to a Roman soldier's low-profile shield. Many of Iceland's volcanoes and Hawaii's Mauna Loa, the world's largest mountain, are shield volcanoes and were formed slowly over time by the quiet effusion of lava without violent eruption. The Hawaiian style of eruption, characterized by jetting fountains of basaltic lava and incandescent rivers of molten rock, is considered the least dangerous type of eruptive activity.

One of the ways cinder cone volcanoes are formed is by mildly explosive Strombolian eruptions that continuously expel slightly more viscous lava and partly molten rock and ash. Stromboli, an island volcano so formed in the Tyrrhenian Sea off the coast of Sicily, gives its name to this type of eruption. Known since classical times as the lighthouse of the Mediterranean, Stromboli erupts with almost clockwork regularity, guiding mariners with ash plumes by day and fire by night. The most famous cinder cone volcano to form in the past century was Paricutín, which unexpectedly sprouted on a cornfield in Mexico following a series of quakes in 1943; it grew 33 feet in its first day, eventually burying its namesake village under a lava flow.

The composite cone, or stratovolcano, is built of lava flows and explosively ejected tephra (volcanic fragments, from the Greek for "ashes"), and is represented by some of history's loftiest and most elegant peaks, including Japan's Mount Fuji, Washington State's Mount Rainier, and Italy's Vesuvius. Composite volcanoes

"We were caught unprepared. We were taking exams when suddenly we heard a very loud explosion. The next thing, we were running as fast as we could. We lost our slippers and got scars and wounds on our feet. I saw with my own eyes the bodies of my villagers. Their families could barely recognize them."

—MOUNT MAYON ERUPTION SURVIVOR MARY CRIS

produce some of the world's most violent eruptions, including those of Mount Tambora in 1815 and Mount Pinatubo in 1990. The force behind this deadly phenomenon is the pyroclastic surge, a term derived from the Greek words *pyro* (fire) and *klastos* (broken) that describes materials formed by the fragmentation of magma and rock by explosive volcanic activity. These flows, sometimes called *nuées ardentes* (French for "glowing clouds") are hot, often incandescent mixtures of volcanic fragments and gases that sweep along close to the ground.

Three eruption types make earth-shattering use of this frequently unpredictable surge. Named for the devastating 1902 lateral blowout of Mount Pelée, on the Caribbean Island of Martinique, a Peléan eruption occurs when thick, sticky masses of lava form a dome over a vent; huge sections of this dome can suddenly break away, sending searing-hot gases and lava fragments racing downslope with hurricane force. Vulcanian eruptions, named for the island of Vulcano, which neighbors Stromboli, are huge gas explosions that unleash magma blocked in a vent by a hardened plug. The most energetic style of eruption bears the name of Roman administrator Pliny the Younger (circa A.D. 62-114), who recorded the events surrounding the devastating eruption of Mount Vesuvius in A.D. 79, which destroyed the towns of Pompeii and Herculaneum. Plinian eruptions eject an enormous ash column 20 miles or more into the stratosphere. Spectacular recent Plinian eruptions include Mount St. Helens in 1980 and Mount Pinatubo in 1991.

PREDICTING CATASTROPHE

In 2006, scientists watching Mount Mayon, the most active volcano in the Philippines, warned locals that the full moon's gravitational pull could trigger an explosive eruption. At least three of Mayon's 50 eruptions over the past 400 years, including the two most recent ones in 2000 and 2001, coincided with the full moon. But the theory that the gravitational pull of sun and moon can influence eruptions remains in dispute.

Still, this theory, if proved, would spell salvation for villagers like Mary Cris, who survived the 1993 eruption of Mount Mayon, which killed 75 people. Cris is from Matanag, a small farming village in the shadow of the volcano, whose constant churning places locals in evacuation limbo. In a BBC news article, Cris spoke of her decision: "I dearly love Mount Mayon," she said. "I never felt sorry of living near its foot despite the danger she brought to our lives. She has given us so much for our living, rich land and water for farming." Crucibles of creation, volcanoes are both destroyers and providers of life. The nutrient-filled ash that volcanoes spew enriches soil and enables farmers to eke out a livelihood on the apron of doom. But just as volcanoes give, they also take away—suddenly and violently.

Unlike meteorology, volcanology is not a predictive science, James Glanz says in a 2003 article in the *New York Times*. "But some scientists cite as predictive such subtle clues as the seismic blips called tornillos that were picked up from Galeras, a volcano in Colombia, before it erupted in 1993 and killed nine people, including six members of a research party."

Scientists can also look at such factors as a volcano's geological profile and history and any deformations of its surface. And earthquakes provide volcanologists with valuable clues, shedding light on the movement of magma.

The developing science of low-frequency sound wave monitoring is especially promising. Unlike earthquakes, which give few warning signs before they strike, active volcanoes broadcast acoustic signals, or infrasound, which travels through the air when the atmosphere is disturbed. Whales and elephants send and hear infrasound across great distances, but these low rumbles are silent to the human ear. This site-specific information is then compared with a database of past

The sketches of William Ascroft capture the spectacular sunsets caused by copious amounts of ash and dust suspended in the atmosphere after the 1883 eruption of Krakatau, in Indonesia.

volcanic activity around the world. Still, confidence in probability estimates can vary. Steve McNutt, a volcano seismologist at the Geophysical Institute of the University of Alaska, Fairbanks, describes such methodology as sometimes resulting in "seat of the pants" estimates. In spite of this, the USGS has been able to predict every eruption of Mount St. Helens since 1980.

Predicting the duration of an eruption is also a challenge, although previous eruptions from a given volcano give an estimate. Eruptions can last anywhere from a day to a year, and some last considerably longer. Hawaii's Kilauea and Italy's Stromboli are just two examples of volcanic eruptions whose durations have exceeded expectations. The former has been erupting since 1983, the latter for some 2,400 years.

DEATH BY VOLCANO

Volcanic eruptions have been among Earth's most cataclysmic events, and for the people confronted with these catastrophes the only appropriate response has been shock, awe, and a burning desire to escape alive. Among the first eruptions to be observed and described with a scientific eye was that of Mount Vesuvius in A.D. 79. Pliny the Elder—who had written, "There can be no doubt that conflagrations are a punishment inflicted upon us for our luxury"—died then, and his nephew, Pliny the Younger, wrote an account of his death and the catastrophe that caused it. According to the history, as thousands fled the darkened city of Pompeii while Vesuvius flung her volcanic bombs, Pliny the Elder, a philosopher of natural history, was drawn ever closer to Vesuvius to watch the "broad sheets of fire and leaping flames" that spelled certain doom for the area around the volcano. As Pliny died, from heart attack or lethal fumes, thousands of others suffocated in a toxic cloud of gas and were buried as deep ash avalanches swept over Pompeii and Herculaneum.

More than 1,500 active volcanoes pockmark Earth's surface; hundreds more lie submerged, and countless others remain dormant or hide in secrecy, waiting their turn to make their devastating debut. On average, a volcano erupts somewhere in the world each week, generally gently, but occasionally with a cataclysmic force greater than the most powerful nuclear bomb. Although volcanic eruptions in history have not produced the mass deaths associated with floods and earthquakes, hundreds of thousands of people have died in volcanic eruptions in the past few centuries, and tens of thousands in the 20th century alone. Seemingly in defiance of the inevitability of deadly volcanic eruption—although most people don't have the option of leaving their volatile landscape—more than 500 million people (about 1 in 12 of the world's population) now live in the danger zones around Earth's active and potentially active volcanoes.

During the spontaneous 1977 fissure eruption of Nyiragongo, in the Democratic Republic of the Congo, a lava lake breached, spawning a lava flow. The

Crime saved Ludger Sylbaris, who miraculously survived the horror of Pelée's murderous explosion while entombed in his subterranean prison cell.

chemical composition of Nyiragongo lava is unusual in that it contains very little silica, making it highly fluid and capable of flowing at great speeds, especially down the volcano's steep upper slopes. This destructive flow sounded the death knell for hundreds of villagers in parts of the Virunga Mountains. But flaming orange lava flows are not the primary culprits in creating casualties. Instead, the forces of eruption turn majestic cones into lethal monsters in a number of surprising ways. Towering columns of ash can collapse, exhaling toxic gases and raining hot rock on the mountain and burying whatever lies below it, as at Vesuvius.

Volcanic landslides, like the debris avalanche at Mount St. Helens in 1980, can unleash devastating lateral blasts. Lahars, mudslides or rivers of water-soaked ash, can smother towns and fields, as they did at Pinatubo, killing hundreds of people and leaving more than half a million homeless. Such landslides and lahars frequently cause more damage and death than the eruptions

"Mount Vesuvius was blazing in several places . . . A black and dreadful cloud bursting out in gusts of igneous serpentine vapor now and again yawned open to reveal long, fantastic flames, resembling flashes of lightning, but much larger . . . Cinders fell . . . then pumice-stones too, with stones blackened, scorched and cracked by fire."

—PLINY THE YOUNGER, LETTER TO TACITUS

Parícutin blasted through the heart of a Mexican cornfield in February 1943. By June, this astonishing volcano looked as if it had been there for eons.

that spawned them. For example, the 1985 blast at Nevado del Ruiz, in Colombia, caused part of the volcano's summit glacier to melt, producing mudflows that raged for more than 50 miles, killing more than 23,000 people. Finally, lava domes can simply collapse on themselves, releasing fast-moving, 1300°F pyroclastic flows—avalanches of hot ash, rock fragments, and gas capable of moving at more than 60 miles per hour.

Fire fountains, ash, dust, rock, lava and pyroclastic flows, mudflows, landslides: What more havoc could an eruption bring? The answers? Gas, lightning, and atmospheric dust. Noxious volcanic gases with strong odors, such as hydrogen sulfide (which smells like rotten eggs), and the acid gases hydrogen chloride and sulfur dioxide (which sting the eyes and throat and eat through clothes) add to the toxic shock and mounting death toll of eruptions. One poisonous gas, hydrogen fluoride, is strong enough to etch glass. And volcanic eruptions can indirectly cause secondary eruptive disasters. In August 1986, a limnic eruption occurred at Cameroon's Lake Nyos, killing more than 1,700 people in villages below the lake. A limnic eruption, or lake overturn, occurs when landslides or volcanic tremors cause carbon dioxide gas to erupt from deep lake water. This silent murderer is particularly dangerous because it usually has no smell; people and animals are asphyxiated by an invisible killer. Such eruptions have been confirmed twice in Cameroon, but may have occurred at least once more. In 1984 Lake Monoun experienced a limnic eruption that asphyxiated 37 nearby villagers. Although rare, such lake overturns are possible wherever a lake becomes saturated, not unlike a carbonated, unopened soda pop can, with volcanically emitted carbon dioxide or gas from decomposed organic material. Central Africa's methane-rich Lake Kivu is now being watched for signs of such an eruption. Yet another brilliant element of volcanic havoc is lightning, which is often seen during eruptions when lava fragments within ash clouds rub against one another and produce static electricity. The electrical charge is released in bolts that leap through the cloud, just as they do in thunderstorms. Lightning that accompanies eruptions makes for a frightful image of raging force.

A DEADLY ATMOSPHERE

But blinding bolts of lightning are mere light shows compared with the dramatic effect that a powerful ashy eruption can have on the weather. In the second century, the Chinese noted unusually red sunrises and sunsets, which were likely to have been caused by volcanic emissions from the huge eruption at Mount Taupo, in New Zealand. Gas and dust from major eruptions can cause dark days, severe winds, and heavy, muddy rains in a local area for months and—if the explosion is powerful enough—send ejecta high into the atmosphere, where it can be carried around the world. Airborne volcanic material brings spectacularly colorful

sunrises and sunsets but can also filter out sunlight and reduce temperatures across the globe. The 1815 eruption at Tambora, in Indonesia, is considered the largest volcanic eruption in modern history. It released ash and sulfur dioxide, which reacted in the atmosphere to form particulates that reduced incoming solar radiation, causing "a year without a summer" across much of the world in 1816. There were summertime frosts in New England, and northern Europe crops were decimated. The eruption directly or indirectly caused the deaths of 92,000 people. In 1783, following large eruptions in Iceland and Japan and decreased solar activity, unusually thick polar ice formed and preceded several unusually cold winters in Europe and America; this event became known as the little ice age.

The Icelandic fissure eruption at Mount Laki brought forth the most voluminous outpouring of lava in recent history. After initial fountains of molten rock and mild explosions hurled tephra skyward, immense floods of extremely fluid basalt burst from a 15-mile-long series of fissures, streaming down river valleys toward the coast. Within two months these flows had buried 226 square miles of pastureland and river ways. Gases released by the Laki eruption were

The 1980 Krafla eruption brings fire to a land of ice and rock. Iceland straddles the Mid-Atlantic Ridge, a fiery seam where two tectonic plates slowly rip apart.

even more destructive to plant and animal life. Forming a bluish haze of sulfur dioxide, a gaseous miasma hovered over the landscape through the summer of 1784, blighting vegetation and stunting crops. Iceland lost roughly 70 percent of its livestock and a fifth of its 49,000 people in the "haze famine" that followed.

JUMP INTO THE FIRE

The ferocity of a volcanic eruption is a terrifying and magnificent display of Earth's internal power. Marco Pinna, a *National Geographic* writer accompanying volcanologists studying Etna's 2001 explosion, described the bubbling lava as making "strident clicking sounds, like glass rubbing glass." In quieter moments, scientists also heard "a dark rumbling below." Carsten Peter, who photographed Etna's eruption, warns: "You must imagine, lava is quite heavy; after all, it's liquid stone flying around." He advises, "You have to stand still, watch where the lava bombs are falling, and get out of the way." *National Geographic*'s Donovan Webster explored the South Pacific island of Ambrym, which was brimming with fire, and returned with terrifying tales of molten visions—"It's mesmerizing: lava

"Through the black, rushing smoke-bursts,
Thick breaks the red flame;
All Etna heaves fiercely
Her forest-cloth'd frame."

—MATTHEW ARNOLD, *EMPEDOCLES ON ETNA*

sloshing back and forth, bubbles emerging and popping like a thick stew."

The deadliest eruption in recorded history is believed to be that of Mount Tambora, in Sumbawa, Indonesia. Between April 12 and 14, 1815, 12,000 people died due to the immediate impact of a series of eruptions, and an additional 80,000 people died as a result of starvation and disease brought on by the explosion. Another famous Indonesian eruption became history's most powerful and second deadliest: Between April 26 and 28, 1883, a series of blasts ripped apart the volcanic island of Krakatau and skyrocketed so much ash into the stratosphere that ships at sea were covered with dust for weeks after the eruption, sunsets were strangely colored, and temperatures around the globe were reduced for more than a year. The roar of its detonation was heard 3,000 miles away—if it had happened in Boston, the detonation would have been heard in both London and Los Angeles. Pyroclastic flows from the first day of Krakatau's eruption killed at least 2,000 people; on the second day, when the volcano's peak collapsed a thousand feet below sea level, the island sank, killing another 3,000 people and triggering a 100-foot-high tsunami that wiped out more than 31,000 people as it crashed over the Indonesian islands of Java and Sumatra.

One of history's most explosive volcanic eruptions, and among the deadliest, was the famous eruption of Vesuvius, near Naples, Italy, at 8:32 a.m. on August 24, A.D. 79, which buried Pompeii and Herculaneum under cinders, ashes, and mud. This massive two-minute blast shook the earth, sent rock, volcanic glass, and steam outward, and triggered a collapse that demolished the cone. A plume of superheated ash was ejected vertically miles into the sky and sparked forest fires. Thousands died and Vesuvius shrank by 1,313 feet in a single day. Pliny the Younger described the Vesuvius eruption, telling of panicked crowds fleeing as their carts were tossed about by earthquakes and of seeing "a horrible black cloud . . . writhing snakelike and revealing sudden flashes rather like lightning." Soon after came tides of falling ash and "the darkness of a sealed room without lights. To be heard were only the shrill cries of women, the wailing of children, the shouting of men."

The deadliest volcanic eruption of the 20th century was the May 8, 1902, eruption of Mount Pelée on Martinique in the West Indies, which killed 29,000 people almost instantly as a result of a nuée ardente, an incandescent, high-velocity cloud of volcanic dust and superheated gases that traveled more than ten miles at speeds of a hundred miles per hour toward the town of Saint-Pierre. Only three citizens survived Pelée's fury, which engulfed the city in flames, incinerating everything in sight, and leaving behind a mournful coating of ash. A

Danger lurks in the Cascades, the volcanic range that runs between northern California and British Columbia. Visitors to Washington's Mount St. Helens compare a photograph of its conical preeruptive profile with a jagged summit produced by its cataclysmic 1980 blowout. Ash blanketed forests and towns following the spectacular eruption, reducing visibility for drivers and making even short journeys perilous.

A man has to stoop to walk through the doorway of his home after the Unzen Volcano in Kyushu, Japan, deposited ash and debris.

number of interesting tales arose from the disaster. Although few paid attention, the "bald mountain" overlooking Saint-Pierre coughed through vent holes and sent local tremors a month before the blast. A week before the eruption, ash rained continuously and the stench of sulfur filled the air. At one point more than a hundred six-foot-long fer-de-lance snakes abandoned their inhospitable homes and invaded Saint-Pierre, killing 50 people and more than 200 animals. On May 5, a landslide of boiling mud had triggered a ten-foot tsunami that killed hundreds. Mount Pelée finally exploded three days later, suffocating the town in fiery volcanic gas and dust. One of the three survivors managed to race from the burning town without breathing the lethal fumes that burned out

The Devil Wears Sulfur

Neither noxious fumes nor unstable ground could keep some thrill-seekers from catching a whiff of Hawaii's eruptive Kilauea.

The Book of Genesis recounts how God "rained down burning sulfur on Sodom and Gomorrah." The Book of Revelation describes the devil's underworld lair as a "lake of burning sulfur" and the Books of Enoch tell of a place of punishment with "rivers of fire" and "a smell of sulfur." Daniel Engber, of *Slate* magazine, writes that "[t]he idea of a sulfurous Hell ruled by an archvillain called Satan seems to have arisen . . . probably in the first or second centuries B.C. . . . By the 400s, the Councils of Toledo would describe him as a horned beast with cloven hooves, a huge phallus, and a sulfurous smell. Tradition placed hell as far as possible from God and heaven. The Bible uses the word 'Gehenna,' which means the 'Valley of Hinnom' and refers to a garbage dump on the outskirts of ancient Jerusalem. Hinnom stood in for the underworld because of its topography—as the lowest point in the area, it served as the spiritual counterpoint for the high ground of the temple mount. The same sort of reasoning imagined hell at the very center of the Earth, in a fiery and sulfurous pit." It stands to reason that if Satan does dwell at the center of Earth, where volcanic activity releases plumes of sulfurous gas in the absence of significant oxygen, then the stench of pure sulfur gas would indeed cling to all the inhabitants of hell.

people's tongues, larynxes, and lungs. Another survivor hid in a cave. And the third survivor, Ludger Sylbaris (also known as Louis-Auguste Cyparis), was saved by the thick stone walls of an underground prison cell to which he'd been confined. Although his back and legs were badly burned, he survived for four days in his accidental fallout shelter until salvage workers rescued him. Sylbaris was pardoned and earned a modicum of fame in carnivals and circuses as "the Prisoner of St. Pierre."

Another notably deadly eruption took place atop Nevado del Ruiz in Colombia, on November 13, 1985. A superheated explosion melted about 10 percent of the volcano's ice cover and caused history's deadliest landslide. A mudslide swept down the volcano's slopes and buried the city of Armero, smothering more than 20,000 people.

Not all eruptions are deadly: The largest volcanic blast of the 20th century took place in 1912 at Novarupta, on the Alaska Peninsula. The blast lasted more than 60 hours and was ten times more powerful than and spewed twice the volume let off by Mount St. Helens in 1980. Earthquakes that preceded the eruption resulted in a mass exodus, and no one was killed, though several villages along Alaska's southeast coast were decimated. On a much smaller scale, the thunderous emergence of the Paricutín volcano in the middle of a Michoacán, Mexico, cornfield on the afternoon of February 20, 1943, was a frightful sight that measured its vengeance in pyroclastic production, not in human lives. Over eight years this cinder cone volcano grew to nearly 1,400 feet and spewed millions of tons of lava across miles of land before concluding its eruption.

The cataclysmic explosion of trapped gases at Mount St. Helens, however, was hardly so subtle; it generated about 500 times the force of the atomic bomb dropped on Hiroshima, belched clouds of hot ash 12 miles into the sky, and reduced the 9,677-foot symmetrical cone by 1,300 feet. In what became the most destructive eruption in U.S. history, giant mudslides, composed of melted snow mixed with ash and propelled by waves of superheated gas erupting out of the crater, rumbled down the slopes and crashed through the valleys, felling millions of trees, blighting 230 square miles of wilderness, and taking 57 lives.

Eleven years later, in April 1991, vigorous steam eruptions, swarms of shallow earthquakes, increased sulfur dioxide emissions, and rapid growth of a lava dome heralded a powerful eruption atop Mount Pinatubo, in the Philippines. As villages were evacuated, a series of small eruptions commenced, quickly leading to a big blow that spewed deadly clouds of 1500°F gas and ash. On June 15, 25-mile-high columns of sulfur dioxide blasted into the atmosphere, the sky turned black from cinders and falling pumice, and earthquakes rattled the ground. Pyroclastic flows swept down the slopes, filling 650-foot canyons and spreading outward as far as 11 miles. The volume of tephra hurled from Pinatubo was so great that it could have buried Washington, D.C., to a level of 150 feet.

The Pinatubo eruption is believed to have been caused when an earthquake the previous year allowed basalt from the upper mantle to squeeze into the magma chamber. The resulting magma rose to the surface, creating a new lava dome. But the mounting pressure was too great, as magma found a conduit to the surface and exploded from the volcano, blasting skyward. Pinatubo's eruption killed nearly 900 people, caused 1.2 million more to be displaced or to lose their livelihoods, and swamped 100,000 acres of cropland with ash. The death toll would have been far greater had scientists not accurately predicted Pinatubo's fury.

And then there are the gentle giants. The difference between an explosive volcano and an oozing one lies in the viscosity and gas content of its magma: Killer volcanoes hold thick, sticky magma and explosive gases under great pressure. Effusive volcanoes hold thinner magma that oozes, flows, and occasionally bursts into fountains. Hawaii Volcanoes National Park, which covers 500 square miles on Hawaii's Big Island, contains two tremendous shield volcanoes: Kilauea and Mauna Loa. According to legend, the fire goddess Pele lives at the bottom of Kilauea's Halema'uma'u crater, although since 1983 she seems to have been expressing her molten fury from the perpetually gushing Pu'u 'O'o crater. Hawaiian volcanoes pour out lava in hot, fast rivers of *pahoehoe* and in a thicker slag called *a'a*. Porous lava nuggets glint green, and nests of volcanic glass called Pele's hair reflect a golden shimmer. "It was like looking back to when the Earth was being born," explains photographer Frans Lanting of his expeditions to the mountain. "Kilauea molds the land, belching lava and fumes, hissing, roaring, always transforming."

Tanzania's Ol Doinyo Lengai is a swirling, oozing, and surprisingly mellow mountain of fire in the Great Rift Valley. This gentle giant is unique in erupting natrocarbonatite lava, a cool, highly fluid lava that creates bizarre formations that erupt at about 1000°F. Ol Doinyo Lengai is Masai for "Mountain of God," and in its own diminutive way, this Vulcanian divinity offers explorers the opportunity to unlock the mysteries of eruption—and have some fun while they're at it. Daring volcanologists frequently climb towering hornitos, extremely sharp and fragile hollow pinnacles that form around active vents, in an active embrace of inner earth's molten nature. Investigations into the interior of a collapsed hornito reveals a lava lake where carbon dioxide bubbles slowly expand and burst, sending aloft silver froth that solidifies in midair and hits the ground with the sound of glass breaking. If only all volcanoes were so subtle and approachable. ■

Electrically charged ash and gas rising from
the volcanic eruption of Indonesia's
Galunggung create a second frightening
phenomenon: lightning.

Even in retrospect, the 1995 temblor that struck Kobe, Japan, is nearly as frightening as the terrifying event itself.

SHAKEN & STIRRED

軽車両を除く

CHAPTER 4

Shaken & Stirred: Earthquakes & Tsunamis

"We learn geology the morning after the earthquake, on ghastly diagrams of cloven mountains, upheaved plains, and the dry bed of the sea."

—RALPH WALDO EMERSON, *THE CONDUCT OF LIFE*

Earth's ceaseless churnings deliver tumult and death, and—despite civilization's timeless protestations and suffering—our planet's terrestrial temper tantrums show no signs of abatement. In 1993, some 10,000 were killed in Latur, India, three years after a 1990 quake in the northwestern corner of Iran cost 50,000 lives. In January 2001, 20,000 people died in India's Gujarat state. In December 2003, a magnitude 6.6 temblor devastated Bam, Iran, smothering more than 26,000 lives. The tsunami of December 26, 2004, spawned by a giant earthquake, extinguished more than 220,000 lives. The magnitude 7.6 quake centered in Kashmir, Pakistan, in October 2005 killed at least 73,000 people and left three million homeless and facing a deadly winter without substantial shelter.

Among the planet's most active fractures, the North Anatolian Fault, which cuts across the Sea of Marmara and slices through Turkey, has caused 13 major earthquakes since 1939. A massive 1999 rupture near Izmit triggered a magnitude 7.6 temblor that shattered cities across northwestern Turkey, leaving tens of thousands dead, 85,000 buildings demolished, and 250,000 homeless. "I've been in many earthquakes, but nothing like this," recalled naval captain Ercüment Dogukanoglu to *National Geographic*'s Rick Gore. "When it hit, I felt helpless—like being thrown every which way in a frying pan."

"MEN ARGUE; NATURE ACTS"

Across the ages—and in many cases not long after a natural catastrophe of unimaginable magnitude has pounded the planet—humans have defaulted to a belief in a

The deadly series of tremors along the North Anatolian Fault in 1999 sent rescue workers scrambling to save lives in Yalova, Turkey.

Oh, miserable mortals! Oh wretched earth!
Oh, dreadful assembly of all mankind!
Eternal sermon of useless sufferings!
Deluded philosophers who cry, "All is well,"
Hasten, contemplate these frightful ruins,
This wreck, these shreds, these wretched ashes of the dead;
These women and children heaped on one another,
These scattered members under broken marble . . .

—Voltaire, from "Poem on the Lisbon Disaster"

great balance of harmonious interdependence in the natural world. From ancient myth and religious parable to Romantic-era philosophy and beyond, examples abound of a momentarily turbulent planet regaining its pristine state—a permanent, perhaps divinely ordained condition that nurtures all life and creates a state of blissful accord. Cicero, Roman orator from the first century B.C. expressed this idea well when he said, "Who cannot wonder at the harmony of things, at this symphony of nature which seems to will the well-being of the world?"

Who cannot wonder at the harmony of things? The French Enlightenment philosopher and writer Voltaire, for one. This inquisitive mind, so passionate about unraveling the mysteries of life—both earthly and divine—bore literary witness to the supreme natural cataclysm of his time: the Great Lisbon Earthquake of 1755. The quake struck on All Saints' Day, devoted to memorial services for the dead, and many of the city's 250,000 were in church. Two tremendous shock waves rattled the city to shards and dusty heaps and created a 20-foot tsunami that swept over the harbor, sucking debris, ships, and bodies into the maelstrom. Raging fires soon followed, conflagrating and fanning across the city, incinerating its treasures and smothering its population. More than 60,000 people—perhaps as many as 90,000—died that morning, but the shock rippled across Europe and into Morocco, killing 10,000 more. Tremors were felt as far away as Finland and Barbados.

The destruction of Lisbon—then among the world's richest capitals and a bastion of Catholic piety and enlightened civilization—came as a blow to the century's faith and optimism. "It was as though a massive fracture had occurred in the natural order of things, as though the very clockwork of the universe has run amuck, "writes historian Bryce Walker, who credits the confidence that came with the age of reason—where no natural phenomenon was without explanation, a time when rational thought led to great advances in the sciences—with amplifying the intellectual shock that came with Lisbon's tremors. For the rationality that led to scientific discoveries by Isaac Newton and René Descartes also carried philosophy into the shadier realm of the Optimist school, a set of beliefs that said not only that human beings were capable of discovering all the laws that governed the universe, but also that they would find them to be divinely ordered, harmonious, and good—that, as one philosopher put it, society lives in "the best of all possible worlds." "The Lisbon quake confounded the Optimist philosophers because the event suggested a dark, uncaring force that swept humanity and its works away without regard for goodness or mercy," Walker writes.

Voltaire was among the first thinkers to seize upon the intellectual consequences of the Lisbon event, which he explored both in poem and in his satirical novel *Candide,* whose protagonist survives the tumult, only to ponder the theological implications of such earthly destruction: "Scarcely had they reached the town . . . when they felt the earth tremble beneath them. The sea boiled up in the harbor and broke the ships which lay at anchor. Whirlwinds of flame and ashes covered the streets and squares. Houses came crashing down. Roofs toppled on to their foundations, and the foundations crumbled. Thirty thousand men, women, and children were crushed to death under the ruins. . . . The terrified Candide stood weltering in blood and trembling with fear and confusion. 'If this is the best of all possible worlds,' he said to himself, 'what can the rest be like?'"

NOT THE BEST OF ALL POSSIBLE WORLDS

The inquisitive Roman philosopher Seneca the Younger pondered the causes and consequences of the earthquake that rattled Pompeii and Herculaneum in A.D. 62—17 years before the cataclysmic eruption of Vesuvius—in

Flattened by an earthquake, then inundated by a tsunami, Lisbon was all but destroyed in 1755.

his commentary *Natural Questions.* But even Seneca was late to the earthquake inquiry. For centuries already, the Greeks had sought to understand the origins of tremors in both myth—the traditional belief held that Poseidon, god of the sea, banged the ocean floor with his trident when angry and caused quakes and tsunamis—and scientific theory. In the fourth century B.C., philosopher Aristotle suggested that tremors were caused by unstoppable vapors emanating from Earth. And with millennia of earthquake evidence piled before them, from the tremors (and volcanic blasts) that contributed to the decline of the ancient Minoan civilization in 1600 B.C. to the shakedown of the biblical cities of Sodom and Gomorrah, early earthquake theorists had a lot of explaining to do.

Some of this early documentation has led to interesting propositions: Historians today theorize that a string of earthquakes about 1200 B.C. may explain the sudden, simultaneous end of Bronze Age civilizations of the eastern Mediterranean, including the city of Troy. A shattering quake and its related tsunami inundated the Greek city of Helice in 373 B.C. and may serve as the origin of the legend of Atlantis. Other quakes caused the destruction of Antioch four times (in A.D. 115, 458, 526, 528) and ceaseless damage to the Aegean and Anatolian regions. Justinian, the sixth-century Roman emperor who officially introduced the majestic Hagia Sophia cathedral in Constantinople, prohibited blasphemy and sexual misconduct on the grounds that they prompted earthquakes. This was a prescient prohibition, for in 557 a massive earthquake nearly flattened his unparalled construction.

As early as 780 B.C., the Chinese were keeping lists of earthquakes and questioning their causes. Past civilizations typically explained earthquakes through myths, most of which place the Earth atop a giant animal or god that periodically twitches, causing its burden to shift. Mongolians believed the world was held up by a giant frog that stumbled under its heavy load, causing the ground to shake. Hindu myth positions the planet on the backs of eight enormous elephants. Algonquin Indians placed Earth on the back of a tortoise. An ancient Japanese legend says that earthquakes come from the writhings of a giant catfish, or *namazu,* that lives in the mud beneath the Earth's surface and is restrained from pranks by a watchful deity, Kashima, who keeps a mighty rock on its head. When Kashima is distracted, the namazu thrashes about and the ground trembles. Norse myth ascribes earthquakes to the subterranean shudders of the trickster Loki, who is eternally punished for murdering Balder, god of innocence, beauty, joy, and peace. The gods bound Loki to three slabs of stone (using his son's innards as bindings) and placed a snake over his head so that its venom would pour onto him. Loki's faithful wife sits beside him

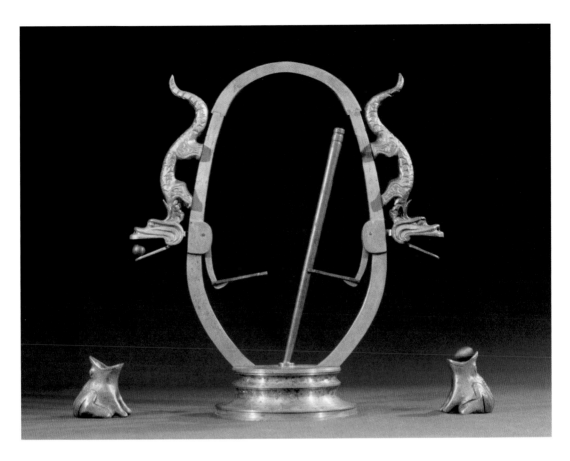

An early seismometer, in which ground tremors caused a bronze ball to drop from a dragon's mouth into a frog's mouth, indicating the direction of the quake△

and collects the venom in a wooden bowl, which she occasionally has to empty, leaving searing venom to drip onto the face of doomed Loki, whose pain is so terrible that he writhes, making the earth shake. In the New World, the pre-Hispanic Chibcha people of Colombia believed that the god Chibchacum, protector of farmers, carried the Earth on his shoulders; earthquakes occurred when he passed the Earth from one shoulder to the other.

Another metaphor for earthquakes comes from personification or projection of human qualities onto the landscape. Myth from Mozambique holds that the Earth is a living creature and has the same kinds of problems people have. Sometimes it gets sick with fever and chills and so trembles. In Inca mythology, Pachamama was a fertility goddess who presided over planting and harvesting and caused earthquakes. Legends from New Zealand tell of Mother Earth protecting a child, the young god Ru, within her womb. His unsettled movements in her womb are experienced by humans as earthquakes. In *Henry IV,* even Shakespeare gets in on the Earth-mother act, envisioning the planet as prone to the fits and discomforts that beset humankind: "Diseased nature oftentimes breaks forth / In strange eruptions; oft the teeming earth/ Is with a kind of colic pinched and vexed / By the imprisoning of unruly wind / Within her womb, which, for enlargement striving, / Shakes the old beldame earth, and topples down / Steeples and moss-grown towers."

FROM FAULTS TO BLAME

What causes earthquakes? A simple scientific explanation would attribute these sudden and terrifying ground tremors to an abrupt shift of rock along a fault, or a fracture in the Earth's surface. But earthquakes can also occur beneath and within volcanoes, and this association offers clues both to the sources of volcanic activity and the fury of shaking ground. As with volcanoes, the vast majority of the world's earthquakes occur around the Pacific Ring of Fire, a 29,825-mile convergence zone that surrounds the Pacific Ocean and is defined by a set of seams where sections of ten massive tectonic plates collide. The boundaries of these plates, which underlie continents and oceans, are defined by belts of seismic activity, and these belts are the clues that formed the basis of the theory of plate tectonics. The forces within the Earth that drive these plate movements result from the cycle of convection currents in the mantle. This

Mapping Seismic Risk

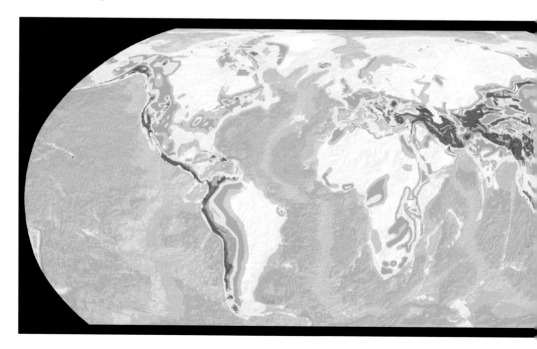

flow of heat forces plates to pull apart (diverge), grind against one another (transform), and collide (converge). Shifting tectonic plates stress rocks along their boundaries, causing folds, domes, and other geologic structures to form in rock layers that create surface landforms such as mountains, cliffs, and valleys. These shifts cause earthquakes.

Although most of the world's great earthquakes take place along well-defined plate boundaries, the theory of plate tectonics does not account for some of history's most violent earthquakes: intraplate tremors, including the New Madrid, Missouri, quakes of 1811-12, which affected the U.S. heartland, states removed from the usual earthquake zones. By the numbers, these temblors are uncommon, and yet their impact is too unnerving to write off. Those experiencing them feel a major shake, followed by a series of gradually weakening aftershocks. The Mississippi Valley quakes, however, were distinguished by three main shocks that radiated out from beneath the quiet town of New Madrid and nearly a year of intermittent aftershocks. The powerful event caused lowlands to flood and created swampland on what had previously been dry land. In Kentucky for one of the shocks, naturalist John James Audubon

"An earthquake achieves what the law promises but does not in practice maintain—the equality of all men."

—IGNAZIO SILONE

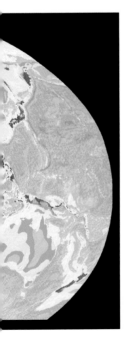

This global map of seismic risk indicates the force of shaking ground and offers a prediction of where quakes are most likely to occur in the future. Areas of highest risk are dark brown and dark red; pink and red indicate high risk; yellow and orange suggest moderate risk; and low-risk areas are white and green.

10 Deadliest Earthquakes in the Past 100 Years

YEAR	LOCATION	DEATHS
1976	Tangshan, China	255,000-655,000
2004	Sumatra, Indonesia	220,000+
1920	Gansu Province, China	200,000
1927	Qinghai, China	200,000
1923	Kanto, Japan	143,000
1948	Ashgabat, Turkmenistan	110,000
1908	Messina, Italy	70,000-100,000
2005	Kashmir	at least 73,000
1932	Gansu Province, China	70,000
1970	Peru	66,000

National Geographic magazine (April 2006)

This rare photograph was taken at the moment that earthquake lights illuminated the sky near Mount Saijo, Japan, after a 1966 temblor.

watched as "all the shrubs and trees began to move from their very roots, the ground rose and fell in successive furrows like the ruffled waters of a lake. The earth waved like a field of corn before a breeze." Mississippi River boat captains were confounded as roiling surf flowed against the river's natural current. Floods and a state of natural dissolution followed. Had this event—which geologists believe originated in a deeply buried rift valley and whose shudders were felt from Canada to the Gulf of Mexico—occurred today, loss of life and property would be devastating. Not on the murderous Lisbon level, perhaps, but life-shattering, nonetheless.

Most earthquakes originate within the top 10 to 20 miles of mantle and crust, the lithosphere, and follow natural faults between two geologic formations. When faults are heavily stressed by tectonic plate collisions or grinding, the fracturing along the edges releases trapped energy, triggering bomb blast–force movement from the hypocenter. As rocks break, seismic (from the Greek *seismos,* or "shock") waves of energy radiate through the Earth and over the surface, causing an earthquake. The point on the surface directly above

the focus is called the epicenter, and this is where ground shaking is typically most severe. Quakes promulgate two kinds of motion at once: fast-moving compressional waves, which speed along at 12,000 to 19,000 mph, and much slower shearing waves. Another, and the most damaging type of wave—the surface wave, which not all earthquakes produce—causes damage to structures by shaking foundations while radiating on the Earth's surface away from the epicenter, much like ripples on a pond. The surface wave is further catagorized by whether the waves radiate vertically—Rayleigh (R) waves—or horizontal-ly—Love (Q) waves. The combination of these two types of waves creates an effect not unike the turbulent surface of the ocean, spelling doom for unstable or tall structures.

Each year roughly 150,000 earthquakes are distinctly noticeable to people near their hypocenter, and more than a million can be detected with instruments such as seismographs. An international network of seismograph stations circles the planet, and by analyzing the time lapse between consecutive primary and secondary waves, scientists can quickly calculate the approximate distance to the source of an earthquake and its location. The invention of the modern seismograph, by which earthquake magnitude is measured from the vibration of a pendulum and duly recorded, dates to the 19th century, but the history of seismography reaches back at least to A.D. 132. The earliest seismometer was the work of Chinese astronomer and mathematician Chang Heng. This device consisted of eight dragons mounted around a six-foot-wide urn encircled by eight toads with gaping mouths; the slightest tremor would shift a pendulum in the urn that would in turn cause a bronze ball to drop from a dragon's jaw into a toad's amphibious maw with a loud clang. When a major earthquake struck the Chinese capital, Luoyang, in A.D. 138, this seismometer alerted its inventor 400 miles away.

The best known measurement of magnitude is the Richter scale, devised in the 1930s and '40s to measure quakes in California, and later adapted for global use. Because the size of earthquakes varies enormously, the Richter scale is not linear but logarithmic; an increase of one in magnitude, therefore, corresponds to a tenfold increase in amplitude—the size of the seismic waves. The bottom end of the Richter scale reflects quakes that are imperceptible to human observers; at its upper end it measures those considered to be catastrophic, but there is no direct correlation between the measurement of a quake and the amount of damage it causes. For example, a quake measuring 9.0 on the Richter scale that strikes in remote ocean waters could have far less of an effect than a magnitude 6.8 quake in a major urban area, such as the one that ravaged Kobe, Japan, in 1995, inflicting extensive damage.

The Earth's movement as the result of a quake depends on the exact location of the epicenter, the underlying ground composition, and the geology of the surrounding earth. The treacherous phenomenon of liquefaction occurs when unconsolidated, wet sediment flows like liquid in response to the seismic waves, with virtually no strength to support structures as the ground heaves. Liquefaction was responsible for much of the damage inflicted by the catastrophic 1989 Loma Prieta earthquake, which struck San Francisco, leaving 63 people dead, nearly 3,800 injured, and more than 28,000 homes and businesses damaged.

Seismographs measure the magnitude of an earthquake, but another important factor—intensity—is based on visible damage to structures, changes on the Earth's surface, and trembles felt. In this way, intensity is a human observation at a specific location, and magnitude is a scientific measurement of the amount of energy an earthquake releases. The Modified Mercalli Intensity scale distinguishes 12 degrees of severity, ranging from I (barely perceptible to humans) to VI (easily perceived by humans, although damage is not significant) to XII (nearly complete destruction—masonry structures leveled, masses of rock

The Call Building in a Maelstrom of Flame – The Great San Francisco Fire completing the devastation of the famous Spreckels' Structure, U.S.A.

The 1906 earthquake that flattened San Francisco initiated an inferno of woe. The Great Quake rattled along an extensive stretch of the San Andreas Fault, destroying city water lines and igniting uncontrollable urban conflagrations that turned city blocks to ash heaps and claimed at least 3,000 lives. The deadliest temblor in U.S. history left more than 225,000 homeless.

The Call–Chronicle–Examiner

SAN FRANCISCO, THURSDAY, APRIL 19, 1906.

EARTHQUAKE AND FIRE: SAN FRANCISCO IN RUINS

NO HOPE LEFT FOR SAFETY OF ANY BUILDINGS

BLOW BUILDINGS UP TO CHECK FLAMES

WHOLE CITY IS ABLAZE

CHURCH OF SAINT IGNATIUS IS DESTROYED

MAYOR CONFERS WITH MILITARY AND CITIZENS

99

LIFE and Death in Fukui, Japan

"At 5:14 o'clock without warning, the floor suddenly pushed up under us, and great chunks of wall and ceiling began to crash about. We staggered for the doors in jerky movements, unable to keep our balance. . . . I was lifted from my feet, tossed sharply aside, and smacked into a wall," scrawled LIFE correspondent Carl Mydans about the cataclysmic onset of the June 28, 1948, 7.3 earthquake that ravaged Fukui, Japan.

Mydans and several other Americans, who had been eating dinner in the mess room of American military headquarters in Fukui, staggered out of the reinforced-concrete building, only to find the world outside in total chaos. "We all tried to lie down," Mydans said, "but the earth shook so violently that some were jerked into a standing position and bounced about like popcorn."

Dispatched to document the city's remarkable recovery from World War II—which had been 97 percent annihilated by Allied firebombs—Mydans expected to photograph a city on the rise. What he witnessed instead was the city's second destruction in three years.

With the first shockwave, all electricity and lines of communication went dead; highways instantly became blocked by mounds of undulating rubble as streets buckled and cracked; train tracks were twisted like putty and wrenched from their beds; and modern buildings, swaying crazily, crumbled and toppled to the ground. Mydans found himself trapped in this city under siege, this time by Mother Nature. At this point, he rushed to get his camera and spent the next 15 hours capturing the horrors of a world gone mad.

Terrified women flee fires in Fukui, Japan, during the 1948 quake captured on film by Carl Mydans.

Moments of silence followed the first devastating tremor. Then "little voices of human beings—cries—rose into a din throughout the city," Mydans reported. Wild winds slapped Fukui with a second, far more devastating blow. "At 5:27 one thin grey wisp of smoke crawled up behind a sagging department store. It grew larger, spreading in all directions."

Although Mydans and the members of the American military team escaped injury, 3,700 Japanese citizens lost their lives. The earthquake dealt the first blow, but the conflagration that ensued was responsible for the horrific death toll.

By the morning following the quake's wrath a road out of the city had been cleared, allowing Mydans's account and pictures to reach the outside world.

displaced). Such complete defeat by Earth's unstoppable forces, which leaves lives and land upturned, can also present scientists with an opportunity to understand our planet's relentless forces of creation, as Charles Darwin reported in March 1835 from the quake-wracked ruins of Concepción, Chile: "It is a bitter and humiliating thing to see works, which have cost men so much time and labour, overthrown in one minute; yet compassion for the inhabitants is almost instantly forgotten, from the interest excited in finding that state of things produced in a moment of time, which one is accustomed to attribute to a succession of ages."

ON SHAKY GROUND

The knowledge gained of quakes and their causes comes from the hard-earned experience of survival, which in turn has produced centuries of discovery that helps explain trembling terrain. But not all observers of natural phenomena can afford to maintain the intellectual detachment that scientists, such as evolutionary theorist Charles Darwin, practiced. Most survivors are just glad to get out alive. One would-be victim of the 1773 earthquake in Guatemala describes his terrifying plight: "We rode on a sea of mountains and jungles, sinking in rubble and drowning in the foam of wood and rock. The earth was boiling under our feet . . . making bells ring, the towers, spires, temples, palaces, houses, and even the humblest huts fall; it would not forgive either one for being high or the other for being low."

The feeling of surviving an earthquake is a mixture of terror and awe— a shock wave blend of sensations that most likely touches millions of people each year. And these are the lucky ones. Earthquakes and related phenomena, such as tsunami and fire, cause thousands of deaths per year worldwide. Some years, and in some specific locations, temblors multiply deaths to an unimaginable level. Earthquakes in Iran in 856 and 893 wiped out some 350,000 citizens. An 1138 earthquake in Aleppo, Syria, claimed the lives of 230,000 people. A massive 1201 earthquake rattled the eastern Mediterranean—Upper Egypt, Syria—and disrupted every major city in the Near East; contemporary estimates put the total number killed by the quake and related events at 1,100,000. And the 1556 temblor in the north-central Shaanxi province killed more than 830,000 people. This tremendous death toll resulted from the collapse of cave homes (or *yaodongs,* carved into the soft cliffs that overlook the Loess Plateau), which buried as much as 60 percent of the region's population alive.

The deadliest earthquake of modern times took place at Tangshan, northern China, on July 28, 1976. Unannounced by foreshocks, a titanic temblor struck at 3:42 a.m., triggering widespread liquefaction and material amplification and

Signs point to utter devastation in Anchorage, Alaska, following the Good Friday Earthquake of 1964.

causing 95 percent of all buildings to collapse, in an instant crushing about 240,000 people—and perhaps more than 655,000, according to unofficial estimates. In seconds this once thriving industrial center was reduced to rubble. Buildings collapsed in rows like dominoes. Thousands of sinkholes appeared, and trees were snapped from the ground. Railroad tracks twisted together, and landslides roared from neighboring hills. And yet the horrors had only just begun. In the following days, a heat wave brought suffocating humidity, followed by incessant rain that flooded lavatories, sewers, and gutters. As unburied bodies putrefied and sanitation conditions festered, outbreaks of dysentery, typhoid, influenza, and encephalitis spread among refugee camps. The Tangshan quake was an unalloyed human catastrophe.

But something interesting happened: The night before the first tremors, a colorful, flashing light display, perhaps caused by the release of underground methane gas, was seen in the sky from as far as 200 miles away. Near the fault line, cornfields and bushes were blown over and burned on one side. It turns out that these glowing, luminescent, multicolored "earthquake lights" have long accompanied some seismological events. The first recorded mention of earthquake lights comes from Callisthenes, who wrote of an earthquake of 373 B.C. that "[a]mong the many prodigies by which the destruction of the two cities, Helice and Buris, was foretold, especially notable were both the immense columns of fire and the Delos earthquake."

As the Tangshan event indicates, the shaking of the Earth is frequently not the greatest danger brought by earthquakes. Catastrophic temblors often open a Pandora's box of suffering that can include raging fires, floods, mudslides, and subsequent disease. The April 18, 1906, Great Quake in San Francisco, which ruptured along a 260-mile section of the San Andreas fault and killed 3,000 people, was the deadliest-ever U.S. quake. In little more than a minute, the earthquake wrecked 490 blocks and toppled more than 25,000 buildings, effectively demolishing the gold rush capital that had stood there for a half century. As related in *Restless Earth,* world-famous tenor Enrico Caruso was in town with New York's Metropolitan Opera when disaster struck. "Everything in the room was going round and round. The chandelier was trying to touch the ceiling, and the chairs were all chasing each other. Crash—crash—crash! . . . Everywhere the walls were falling and clouds of yellow dust were rising . . . I thought it would never stop."

But the shaking did cease, and the greatest damage came from the fires that followed, fanning out from overturned stoves, broken gas mains, and damaged electrical wiring. Fifty fires were reported within 15 minutes of the quake, and 6 hours after the first tremors, a square mile in the heart of the city was aflame. During the next three days the urban conflagration raged, creating a firestorm

Witness to devastation, a partially buried photograph presents a grim portrait of the December 26, 2003, earthquake that turned Bam, Iran, into a city of ruins.

Tsunami Waves

Fault or earthquake

Undersea landslides, volcanic eruptions, and earthquakes can cause ocean waves to radiate in widening circles. In the open sea, tsunami waves barely ripple the surface. As they reach shallower water, however, these surging waves slow down, pile up, and become liquid mountains that crash onto land with furious force.

Ten Worst Tsunamis

Location	Date	Death Toll
Southeast Asia	Dec. 26, 2004	287,534
Krakatau, Sumatra/Java	Aug. 27, 1883	36,380 *
Sanriku, Japan	June 25, 1896	28,000
Agadir, Morocco	Feb. 29, 1960	12,000 **
Lisbon, Portugal	Nov. 1, 1755	10,000
Papua New Guinea	July 18, 1998	8,000
Chile/Pacific Islands/Japan	May 22, 1960	5,700
Philippines	Aug. 17, 1976	5,000
Hyuga to Izu, Japan	Oct. 28, 1707	4,900
Sanriku, Japan	March 3, 1933	3,000

*Combined effect of volcanic eruption and tsunamis
**Combined effect of earthquake and tsunamis

Source: Russell Ash, *The Top 10 of Everything*: 2006, DK Publishing, 2005

that ultimately consumed 28,000 buildings. Steel and glass were no match for the 2000°F temperatures, and some buildings even exploded from the pressure, rather than waiting to be engulfed in flame. Witness to the horror, novelist Jack London turned to his pen to record the event: "It was dead calm," he wrote. "Not a flicker of wind stirred. Yet from every side wind was pouring in upon the city. . . . The heated air rising made an enormous suck. Thus did the fire of itself build its own colossal chimney through the atmosphere. Day and night the dead calm continued, and yet, near to the flames the wind was often half a gale, so mighty was the suck." The last threatening blaze finally died down about three days after the Great Quake, having reduced more than four square miles of the west's grandest metropolis to ash.

"The dead and the injured were everywhere. Some had been crushed by falling buildings; some had been engulfed by flames. Others were trampled to death by hordes of people and animals. Many people, stranded inside and on the roofs of burning buildings jumped," writes Carol Orsag Madigan. "In one case, a policeman and several citizens tried in vain to free a man buried under burning wreckage. As one of the rescuers later said: 'The helpless man watched in silence 'til the fire began burning his feet. Then he screamed and begged to be killed. The policeman took his name and address and shot him through the head.'"

The quake that rattled Fukui (page 100) was just one in a timeless chain of calamities that have shaken and stirred Japan over the centuries, including the murderous Great Kanto Earthquake of 1923, an awful tremor that killed 143,000 people in Tokyo and the surrounding Kanto Plain. A more recent disaster was the Great Hanshin Earthquake of January 17, 1995, which struck near Kobe—Japan's second most important port—and constituted the worst calamity to hit Japan since World War II. The quake killed more than 6,400 people, injured thousands more, damaged 190,000 buildings, toppled bridges, twisted highways, snapped trucks like toothpicks, and scrambled water, gas, and electrical services for months. Although most deaths resulted from collapse of wood-frame and stucco houses—atop loose soil that amplifies the effects of seismic waves and is prone to liquefaction—the temblor also caused widespread building failure where it was least expected: in newer, "earthquake-proof" structures, such as the Hanshin Expressway, whose supports crumbled.

The quake raised doubts about Japan's earthquake preparedness, as well as researchers' attempts at prediction. "Three years ago I proudly declared, 'In Japan, highways will never collapse,'" Toshio Mochizuki, one of Japan's leading authorities on anti-earthquake measures told *National Geographic* at the time. "I now realize how naïve I was."

Poorly built structures largely account for the 17,000 deaths brought on by the August 1999 earthquake in Izmit, Turkey, and the shattering 2005 shudders

Birds, Snakes, and Bunny Rabbits:
Can animals sense earthquakes and tsunamis?

"Some of the simplest questions about earthquakes remain hard to answer," writes Joel Achenbach in *National Geographic*. "Why do they start? What makes them stop? Does a fault tend to slip a little—telegraphing its malign intent—before it breaks catastrophically? Why do some small quakes grow into bigger quakes, while others stay small?" Alas, earthquake prediction remains stubbornly complex, and answers to even the most basic questions about seismic stress can lead down dark corridors of scientific uncertainty.

Maps of fault zones serve as the basis for forecasts and offer some insight to the inner workings of our planet, but even these seem an echo of the reports of peculiar behavior by animals before earthquakes that have come from many parts of the world. In China, frightened rats and dogs helped predict a major earthquake in Liaoning Province in 1975. Chickens flew up in trees and screeched loudly. Cats picked up their kittens in their mouths and ran for their lives. It is believed that the animals had noticed tiny tremors and rising gases that were undetected by humans. Officials ordered an evacuation of the city, and when the earthquake finally hit, citizens were camping safely in the fields outside the city.

"The belief that animals can predict earthquakes has been around for centuries," says National Geographic's Maryann Mott. "In 373 B.C., historians recorded that animals, including rats, snakes and weasels, deserted the Greek city of Helice in droves just days before a quake devastated the place. Accounts of similar animal anticipation of earthquakes have surfaced across the centuries since. Catfish moving violently, chickens that stop laying eggs and bees leaving their hive in a panic have been reported. Countless pet owners claimed to have witnessed their cats and dogs acting strangely before the ground shook—barking or whining for no apparent reason, or showing signs of nervousness and restlessness." Although it is not certain why animals behave this way, it is possible they are much more sensitive to their environment than humans and can actually sense movement, electrical changes, or gas emissions.

Researchers all over the world have long studied animals in hopes of discovering what they hear or feel before the earth shakes to use that sense as a prediction tool. One study of animal reactions before major tremors, including the Northridge, California, quake in 1994 and the Greek and Turkish quakes in 1999, documented peculiar behavior beforehand, such as otherwise stable housepets exhibiting signs of stress: cats taking cover, dogs yowling inconsolably, and caged birds becoming agitated. Complicating the matter is the fact that Chinese scientists have learned that not all earthquakes cause unusual animal behavior. Most American seismologists, meanwhile, tend to be skeptical, and many geologists dismiss these reports as "the psychological focusing effect," where people remember strange behaviors only after an earthquake or other catastrophe has taken place. So more research is needed before a reproducible connection between animal behavior and the occurrence of a quake can be made.

that killed at least 73,000 in Kashmir. The December 26, 2003, temblor in Iran flattened the world's biggest adobe structure, the Bam Citadel, and most of the city around it, bringing death to tens of thousands of people. But some quakes are simply so powerful that no amount of preparation can protect those in harm's way. The most powerful earthquake ever recorded exploded off the coast of Chile in 1960. The magnitude 9.5 temblor killed more than 2,000 and left more than two million homeless. This event generated a tsunami that caused death and destruction as far away as Hawaii, Japan, and the Philippines. The second most powerful quake of the 20th century rocked Alaska on March 27, 1964, for about four minutes, causing widespread damage and death. This Good Friday Earthquake was the most powerful quake in U.S. history and took 125 lives. Tremors caused landslides and ocean floor shifts that generated fierce tsunamis.

Where landslides are concerned, few earthquakes can compare with the gruesome horror brought on by the May 31, 1970, Ancash temblor in Peru,

More than 22,000 people died in the tsunami that hit the Japanese island of Honshu in 1896. This woodblock print records a watery sorrow that has become a repeat offender on Honshu.

which destabilized the northern wall of Mount Huascarán, triggering an avalanche of 80 million cubic yards of rock, mud, and snow. A wall of debris one mile long, half a mile wide, and half a mile deep hurtled through the towns of Ancash, Ranrahirca, and Yungay at more than 100 miles per hour, completely burying the towns, killing more than 70,000 people, and leaving tens of thousands homeless.

Mateo Casaverde, a Peruvian geophysicist, was an eyewitness to the Huascarán avalanche:

> As we drove past the cemetery in Yungay the car began to shake. We immediately got out and I saw several homes as well as a small bridge crossing a creek near Cemetery Hill collapse. After a half minute the shaking began to subside . . . and I heard a giant roar coming from Huascarán. Looking up I saw what appeared to be a wave, a cloud of dust, and it looked as though a large mass of rock and ice was breaking loose from the north peak. My immediate reaction was to run for the high ground. The crest of the wave had a curl, like a huge breaker coming in from the ocean, at least 80 meters high. I reached the upper level of the cemetery just as the debris flow struck the base of the hill. I was probably only 10 seconds ahead of it.

Caught in the moment: A photograph taken as six tsunamis rolled across the sands of Krabi in southern Thailand, on December 26, 2004

Mudslides, landslides, lahars, and avalanches are deadly torrents of debris brought down by the predictable agents of slope, mass, and gravity—and the random impetus of quake, eruption, heat, wind, rain, or bad luck. Around the world each year about 150 people are killed by snow avalanches, with the slippery, steep Alps of Switzerland typically chalking up the most fatalities. This is little surprise to students of history. Avalanches in the Alps have been recorded for more than 2,000 years. In 218 B.C. nearly half of Hannibal's 38,000-strong army perished when crossing these ferocious passes. Many died in avalanches. On December 13, 1916, more than 10,000 people died when snows rolled over the Tyrol region of the Italian-Austrian Alps. Fatal and fantastic avalanches and landslides have claimed thousands of lives around the world, from Europe to Asia and North America. The treacherous Andean slopes of South America—from Chile to Peru, Ecuador, Colombia, and Venezuela—account for a staggering number of deaths caused by plummeting debris.

Moving north along the Ring of Fire, the crashing of crustal plates in 1976 killed 23,000 people in Guatemala; contributed to the eruption of Mexico's El Chichón volcano in 1982; and claimed 10,000 lives in earthquakes that struck Mexico City on two consecutive days in 1985. In 1989 the San

Speedy Shock Waves

The December 26, 2004, Sumatra earthquake that generated the titanic tsunami occurred along a highly active subduction zone and created shock waves of energy that radiated from the temblor's hypocenter and crossed the Indian Ocean in a matter of hours, reaching Africa's east coast within half a day.

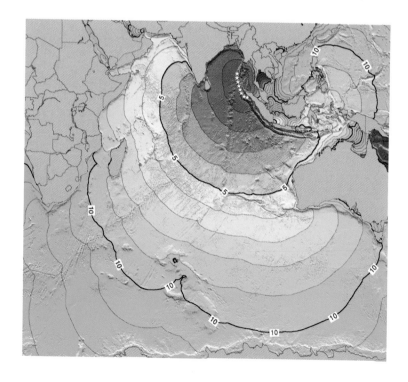

Francisco Bay area was stuck in a blender for 15 terrifying seconds by the magnitude 7.1 Loma Prieta temblor, which struck just before the third game of the World Series (Giants versus Oakland). The quake was triggered when a 30-mile-long segment of the San Andreas Fault abruptly shifted; tremors were felt across a million square miles, from Los Angeles to Oregon, and when the vibrations faded, 63 persons lay dead or dying, and 28,000 houses and businesses faced demolition. The worst loss of life occurred along Interstate 880 in Oakland, where 44 slabs of concrete deck, each weighing 600 tons, pancaked vehicles below. In 1994, nine Los Angeles highways buckled and warped and 60 people died when a 30-second quake vexed Northridge, a suburb of Los Angeles. More than a thousand aftershocks kept the ground shaking long after the big bang.

TSUNAMIS: WATERY GRAVES

A colossal tragedy of our time, the December 26, 2004, Indian Ocean earthquake and tsunami, which annihilated more than 220,000 lives, did not come unannounced—at least if you were paying attention to what the animals were doing. The event was heralded by all manner of animal behavior: Dogs cowered indoors; elephants trumpeted as they headed, literally, for the hills; flamingos fled their typical breeding areas in regions that would soon be vulnerable to the giant waves that pummeled the shores of Sri Lanka and India. Although the massive tsunami triggered by a magnitude 9.0 temblor between the Australian and Eurasian plates off the coast of northern Sumatra killed tens of thousands of people in more than a dozen countries, relatively few animals were reported dead. But this fact comes as little consolation to the world wrecked by these unstoppable moving walls of hundreds of billions of tons of thundering foaming green and black water.

A tsunami—from a Japanese word meaning "harbor wave"—is a series of great sea waves caused by an underwater earthquake, landslide, or volcanic eruption. Submarine landslides or vertical fault movement can cause a massive displacement of water, which in turn produces a powerful series of seismic sea waves that can travel like a freight train across open expanses of water. Tsunami waves can extend 60 miles, land as far as one hour apart, and carry most of their force across vast distances of ocean. For example, even after traveling for 3,000 miles, the Indian Ocean tsunami still slammed hard enough into Africa to kill and destroy. In deep ocean, a tsunami can blast along at 500 miles per hour, invisible except for a one-foot wave and unnoticeable to sailors. As the waves approach land, however, their lower portions drag along the shallow ocean floor, slowing, as the crest grows to dramatic heights. The highest tsunamis on record rose to hundreds of feet, sweeping through the Ryukyu

A survivor surveys a devastated village in Kajhu, in the Indonesian province of Banda Aceh, more than three months after the tsunami obliterated the region.

Islands south of Japan in 1971, Siberia's Kamchatka Peninsula in 1737, and Alaska's Lituya Bay in 1958.

Because lands near the Ring of Fire experience the majority of the world's earthquakes and eruptions, this massive area is also prone to tsunamis, particularly along the coasts of Alaska, Russia, Japan, the Philippines, Indonesia, and western South and Central America. The most damaging tsunami on record before 2004 was the one that killed an estimated 40,000 people in 1782 following an earthquake in the South China Sea. Over the past 1,200 years, Japan has been smashed by at least 70 tsunamis, which have carried away more than 100,000 lives. In northern Chile more than 25,000 people were killed by a tsunami in 1868. In 1883, some 36,500 people were killed by tsunamis in the South Java Sea, following the eruption of Indonesia's Krakatau volcano.

Four wrecking ball sea waves accounted for the vast majority of deaths and the devastation of 165 villages on the coasts of Java and Sumatra in the aftermath of Krakatau's eruption. "Of all the victims whose death can be attributed directly to volcanic activity during the last 250 years, fully a quarter are now believed to have died—drowned or smashed to pieces—as a result of the gigan-

tic waves that were created by the eruptions," notes Simon Winchester, author of *Krakatoa: The Day the World Exploded.* "The entire Minoan civilization on Crete was supposedly wiped out in 1648 B.C. when volcanic tephra from the eruption of Santorini—or, much more probably, the tsunamis thrown up by the eruption—destroyed the palaces at Knossos. More than ten thousand people died in 1782 in the waves that were created by an avalanche of volcanic debris that hurtled into the sea from Japan's Mt. Unzen. In 1815 a similar number of Javanese died when Tambora exploded, sending pyroclastic flows raging into the ocean, with tsunamis radiating out in all directions and inundating the coast."

TSUNAMI OF THE CENTURY

The lightning-fast 2004 Indian Ocean tsunami created waves of only about a foot but moved faster than a commercial jet, peaking at about 30 feet as it reached shallow coastal waters. In one of history's most destructive disasters, these seismic waves first crashed over Indonesia's Aceh Province within 15 minutes of the initial tremors. The Andaman Islands were struck within 30 minutes, southern Thailand within 90 minutes, Sri Lanka within 2 hours, the Maldives within 3.5

hours, and the coast regions of Somalia, on the African continent, in about 7 hours. Tragically, coastal areas received no warning of the impending doom—even on such distant shores as Sri Lanka, which could have initiated massive evacuations within the two hours before the waves struck. The only sign came just before the waves crashed, when the waterline suddenly retreated, exposing hundreds of feet of beach and seabed. The several tsunami waves came at intervals of between 5 and 40 minutes; in some areas the water reached inland half a mile, delivering destruction and death to unprepared locals and vacationers.

"I was sunbathing with my girlfriend on the beach in Phuket [Thailand] when suddenly I heard an unbelievably loud roar, it sounded like I was standing next to an airplane as it took off. I looked up and found a 20-foot high wall of water coming at me—it looked like a scene from the Ten Commandments," reported Vijay Patel to CNN.com. "My girlfriend and I just got up and started running for our lives. The water caught up to us and briefly pulled us under before we surfaced and somehow managed to hold onto a utility pole. Finally the water subsided and we were able to make it uphill to safety. We saw at least 25 bodies float by." Abhishek, of Chennai, India, offered an even more harrowing account to the news site: "I witnessed the most horrible scene in my life: people running for their lives, dead bodies on the road, mothers crying. I've never seen anything like this in my life. Entire fishing villages have been wiped out, huge cars floating. The bodies of children no older than seven are lying on the beach."

The Indian Ocean tsunami left behind a changed world. "The best way to describe this—because we grew up with the images and we all know what it looked like—is that Banda Aceh looks like Hiroshima after the atomic bomb," explained *National Geographic* photographer Chris Rainier, who was working as a relief volunteer. Banda Aceh, on the island Sumatra, was only 155 miles from the earthquake's epicenter. "The buildings have been flattened for miles and entire communities have been swept out to sea. It's day 15 since the disaster, and still there are vast areas where exposed bodies can be seen lying around, decaying. Just cleaning up, picking up the bodies, remains the biggest challenge," Rainier said.

In July 2006, a six-foot-high tsunami hit the south coast of the island of Java, Indonesia, killing at least 668 people. "I saw enormous waves engulf our beach and sweep away cars and boats," eyewitness Elan Jayalani told BBC News. This recent event may not compare in scale with the 1755 calamity that brought death to Lisbon and inspired Voltaire to write *Candide,* but it powerfully demonstrates again the ceaseless tumult civilization faces as it continues surfing on a series of plates that crash into one another billions of years after the planet formed. ■

Villagers in Nam Kem, Thailand, look at a boat swept inland along with debris during the 2004 Indian Ocean tsunami.

Hurricane Georges generated 90-mile-per-hour winds that battered Houseboat Row, in Key West, Florida, on September 25, 1998.

STORMY
WEATHER

CHAPTER 5

Stormy Weather:
Tempests and Watery Graves

Do you know what it means to miss New Orleans,
And miss it each night and day?
I know I'm not wrong, this feeling's gettin' stronger
The longer I stay away.
Miss them moss-covered vines, the tall sugar pines
Where mockin' birds used to sing
And I'd like to see that lazy Mississippi hurryin' into spring

—LOUIS ARMSTRONG, "DO YOU KNOW WHAT IT MEANS TO MISS NEW ORLEANS"

Devastation came to New Orleans with apocalyptic swiftness when Hurricane Katrina unleashed her torrential fury in August 2005. In five terrifying hours the costliest natural disaster in American history laid waste to the Gulf Coast, delivering gusts that peaked at 125 miles per hour; generating 20-foot storm surges that submerged cities in Alabama, Mississippi, and Louisiana and pouring rain that inundated towns and cities; and forcing federal officials to issue disaster declarations that covered 90,000 square miles. All told, Katrina flattened 150 miles of coastline, caused more than $80 billion in damage, delivered tornadoes and floods that brought death to at least 1,836 people in seven states, making this the deadliest hurricane since the 1928 Okeechobee event. Wide-ranging destruction defined this storm, which battered Gulfport, Slidell, Biloxi, Pass Christian, and dozens of other cities and towns along the Gulf Coast. But by far the force of Katrina's fury was reserved for one city: New Orleans.

Founded in 1718, the funky port city that gave birth to jazz and reminded visitors to *laissez les bon temps rouler* at Mardi Gras has always been vulnerable to the currents of the Mississippi River and the rising waters of Lake Pontchartrain. For visitors and residents alike, the Crescent City represented an alternative America, a Francophone-Acadian-Creole blend of European and Caribbean cultures charged by a racy Cajun-spiced streak of permissiveness. Tourists flocked to Bourbon Street for scandalous escapades and toured the graceful Garden District for atmospheric escapes. The below–sea level city had weathered its share of invasions, storms, and floods, but none prepared it for the cataclysm called

Death-defying photographer Mike Theiss captures Hurricane Katrina's massive storm surge as rising water overtakes a beachfront hotel in Gulfport, Mississippi, on August 29, 2005.

Katrina, in which a Category 4 hurricane-fueled storm surge initiated a civil engineering disaster of epic proportions. The U.S. Army Corps of Engineers built floodwalls, but they were no match for the surge, and 80 percent of the city flooded. Although the vast majority of residents had evacuated, tens of thousands stayed behind, determined to weather the storm. Hundreds of people died in the inundation or in their desperate attempt to reach shelters like the Superdome.

The water surges that swamped 100,000 homes in New Orleans exposed the poverty in the low-lying areas of the metropolis. In the days that followed the flood, residents reported seeing bodies lying in the street or floating by in polluted, receding waters. Searing heat rotted the flesh of undiscovered, housebound victims into a putrid, pungent stew. Exhausted relief crews slowly collected the dead as they maneuvered around the downed electric cables, fallen trees, and mud-filled cars that littered streets and sidewalks. The material debris left in the wake of destruction boggled the imagination. "Catastrophe feeds the dump," noted American novelist John Updike, reviewing a book of post-Katrina photographs in the *New York Review of Books.* "Heaped onto the street and sidewalk are tons of the flimsy stuff of American housing—fiberglass insulation like poisonous cotton candy; sheets of warped plywood; mock-pine pressed sheathing; pulverized plasterboard; aluminum siding splayed like palm fronds as houses floated and twisted; strips of metal and molding; plastic-covered shelves and countertops; shower curtains and mattresses, downspouts and lawnmowers, air conditioners and refrigerators mired in a state of eternal paralysis."

Assyrian wind demon Pazuzu, depicted in this eighth-century-B.C. figure, personified storms, pestilence, and disease.

Katrina will be remembered both for its widespread physical destruction and, more profoundly, for the human tragedy it brought: the lives it extinguished and the world it cast asunder. More than just levees broke—the spirit of lifelong locals broke as well. "No words can describe the sense of hopelessness that engulfs you upon entering this region—how tiny you feel in the wake of the immense power that wipes one home from the earth, yet allows a small tree to hold its ground 20 feet away," wrote Army Capt. Steve Alvarez, who reported on the disaster in American Forces Press Services. "There is no eloquent way to package this—no way to couch it into a talking point, into a theme, into a message. The word 'catastrophe' doesn't even rate what Katrina has done here. We need to find a new word for this level of devastation, coin something to capture this horror. . . . Hurricane Katrina is no more, but like all violent acts she has left an indelible scar on victim and relief worker alike. I am not a victim of Katrina, but I still feel the intensity of fear and immensity of loneliness that survivors here feel." The hurricane horror of August 2005 will most likely go down as one of the nation's most spectacular disasters—a natural disaster compounded by human error and misfortune on a monumental level. An estimated 200,000 displaced citizens will never return to New Orleans. That's hard news to take, especially for a city as vibrant as the Big Easy.

BLASTS FROM THE PAST

Merciless, inconvenient, rude, dangerous, unforgiving, deadly: Although only a few natural disasters in U.S. history can compare with the Katrina catastrophe, that cataclysm is just one in an endless string of global weather-related rampages. History, myth, folklore, and literature are littered with extreme events that have changed the course of history. In an instant, hurricanes, rainstorms, windstorms, lightning strikes, floods, tornadoes, and blizzards can irreversibly alter the shape of our planet and the lives of millions of people. And yet, unlike volcanic eruptions and earthquakes—which can ravage with no warning whatsoever—storms are visible and evolving, emerging from a string of clues that offer the tantalizing promise of predictability. A promise, alas, that across the ages goes unheeded or unrealized, often with catastrophic results.

Wayward weather has forever plagued humankind, from biblical floods to the 17th-century dry spell that fueled London's Great Fire in 1666—"every thing, after so long a drought, proving combustible, even the very stones of churches," noted Samuel Pepys. In 1846, wet conditions wiped out all of the potatoes in Ireland, a blight leading to devastating famines that killed off thousands. Archaeologists have speculated that a dry spell from 1276 to 1299 forced the Anasazi Indians of the American Southwest to abandon their homes in serach of water. In 1566, Bishop Diego de Landa documented in vivid detail a deadly storm—perhaps the earliest reported hurricane in the New World—that had wracked Mexico's Yucatán Peninsula generations before his arrival. "During a winter's night, about six o'clock in the evening, there arose a wind which kept increasing and soon changed into a hurricane of four winds. This wind overthrew all the large trees causing a great destruction of every kind of game; and it destroyed also all the tall houses which, since they were covered with straw and contained fire on account of the cold, they burned up a large part of the people."

"An earthquake, a landslip, an avalanche, overtake a man incidentally, as it were—without passion. A furious gale attacks him like a personal enemy, tries to grasp his limbs, fastens upon his mind, seeks to rout his very spirit out of him."

—JOSEPH CONRAD, *TYPHOON*

Fish, Frogs, and Flying Horses:
Weird Weather and the Tornado Effect

"Nature is powerful. On occasion it also can be incredibly weird," writes climatologist Randy
Cerveny, who has turned his teeming database of 8,000 bizarre weather events—including
luminous snowfalls, blood rains, ball lightning, bug snows, flying cows, killer hail, Mid East
snowfalls, waterspouts, and windstorms—into the fascinating compendium *Freaks of the Storm:
From Flying Cows to Stealing Thunder: The World's Strangest True Weather Stories*. "In times past,
newspapers rushed to press with stories sensationalizing the 'freaks' of the latest tornado,
hurricane, or lightning strike. Occasionally, that rush to supply public curiosity led to huge
exaggeration." Examples:

- October, 1947: Hundreds of fish fell from the sky around the town of Marksville,
  Louisiana.

- November, 1915: A tornado ripped through Great Bend, Kansas, blasting five horses a
  quarter mile from their barn; they landed unhurt and still hitched to the same rail. As
  many as 45,000 migrating ducks were found dead; battered ducks fell from the sky
  40 miles away. Residents found an iron water hydrant full of splinters. A dresser from
  a destroyed home was demolished, but its fragile mirror was discovered unbroken
  against a fence.

- Long Island, 1938: The Great Hurricane of 1938 wreaked havoc along the Eastern
  Seaboard and left behind some oddities: residents discovered chickens with their
  feathers plucked completely by the wind. A small cottage was swept away by a wave
  and deposited hundreds of yards away—upside down, yet unbroken.

Fortean, a word frequently used to describe weird weather events, honors the legacy of
Charles Fort, a pioneer documenter of eccentric and exotic phenomena. Among his favorite
bizarre science topics were reports of falling fish and frogs, including a tremendous storm of
two-month-old toads near Toulouse, France, in 1804; a London frog storm in 1838; a famous
1859 fish fall at Mountain Ash in Glamorganshire; one of the heaviest deluges of fish on record in
India in 1850; a fall of hundreds of sand eels in Hindon, England, in 1918. Cerveny writes: "As
potential explanation for such events as falling fish and frogs, [Fort] suggested that a vast ocean
orbits in space near Earth, a 'Super-Sargasso' space sea filled with odd creatures and materials

The howling wind blasts of a tornado have the power to propel light objects, such as this vinyl record, through dense surfaces, such as a telephone pole.

that, as he put it, occasionally has its bottom 'dropped out.' It is debatable as to whether Fort actually believed his hypothesis, was trying to be amusing or tongue-in-cheek, or, by suggesting such an absurd idea, was heaping scorn and disdain onto traditional science."

Extreme weather at times even seems to challenge the very laws of physics. Stories abound of straws and other light objects being hurled by tornadic gales into hard objects such as telephone poles. But how can light and relatively soft objects be forced to impale hard, heavy ones? The straw's shape and the speed at which the tornado is causing it to move allow it to become embedded when kinetic energy focuses on its tip and, for a brief period of time, the straw can overcome the strength of the pole's surface.

Regional Hair-Raisers

Gulf Streams, jet streams, trade winds, and powerful aeolian winds—hurricanes and tornadoes that produce geological change—get all the attention, but dozens of local wind systems have their own names as well. Behold a bunch of breezily named blowers.

Abroholos	Squalls that occur from May through August between Cabo de São Tome and Cabo Frio on the coast of Brazil.
Chinooks	These "snow eaters" are dry foehn winds that melt snow where the Canadian Prairies and Great Plains end and the Rocky Mountains begin. They are named for the regional Chinook Indians.
Diablos	Hot, dry offshore winds from the northeast that typically occur in the San Francisco Bay Area during spring and fall.
Elephanta	Winds that mark the end of the southwest monsoon on the west coast of India.
Etesian	The Greek name for a northerly wind that gusts across Greece and Turkey. Turks call it the Meltemi.
Foehn	A type of warm, dry wind that occurs when a deep layer of prevailing wind is forced over a mountain range. The original is named for a southerly off the northern side of the Alps.
Haboob	A strong wind that stirs up sandstorms in the Sudan.
Harmattan	This dry northerly wind races across central Africa.
Mistral	An atmospheric phenomenon that creates a cold, strong northwesterly wind along the coast of southern France and in Sardinia, Italy. It is said to make people crazy.
Nor'easter	Hurricane-force winds off the east coast of North America, delivering heavy snow, rain, and tremendous waves.
Nor'wester	A bad-tempered wind that brings rain to the west coast and warm, dry air to the east coast of New Zealand.
Papagayo	Violent autumnal northeasterly that whips Pacific Central America.
Pineapple Express	Warm, humid air that wafts across the Pacific Ocean from Hawaii to California and the Pacific Northwest.
Santa Anas	These "murder winds" (named for the migraines and psychosis they are said to cause) are warm, dry winds that appear in Southern California during autumn and early winter. Foehn winds, Santa Anas are caused by pressure buildup in the Great Basin between the Sierra Nevada and the Rocky Mountains.
Shamal	Northwesterly summer wind over Iraq and the Persian Gulf.
Simoom	A strong, dry, desert wind that zips across the Sahara, Palestine, Jordan, Syria, and the desert of Arabia.
Sirocco	Dry, hot North African air from the Sahara; scatters sand, storms to the Mediterranean, and cold wetness to Europe.
Squamish	Cold polar air that funnels into British Columbia fjords.
Vendevale	This westerly wind billows into the Mediterranean Sea around the area of the Straits of Gibraltar and Morocco.
Williwaw	Blasts from the mountains to the sea in the Aleutian Islands and the Straits of Magellan.
Zonda	A fast, dry foehn wind that often occurs on the eastern slope of the Andes in Argentina.

Wet and dry, fire and rain, gale-force winds and ominous hushes. The ancients frequently interpreted weather as a divine reward or punishment. Egyptian communities appeased Set, the god of storms, to withhold desert storms. The ancient Greeks, ruled by a thunderbolt-wielding Zeus, identified four chief winds called Anemoi and ascribed their power to breezy gods. Boreas, the north wind, sent a cyclone to destroy King Xerxes' attacking navy in 480 B.C. The word *zephyr,* or "gentle breeze," comes from Zephyrus, the west wind, who was said to have sired the immortal horses of Achilles, from Homer's Iliad. To the Greeks, Notus was the south wind and Eurus was the east wind. In Greco-Roman myth, Aeolus was the ruler of all winds; the Aeolian harp produces musical chords when breezes caress its strings. The Greeks believed that Aeolus kept the winds in a cave with a dozen holes, all blocked by stones. When he wanted a wind to blow from a certain direction, he rolled away the stone controlling that wind. To create a hurricane, Aeolus opened all 12 holes. On his return to Ithaca from the Trojan War, Odysseus lands at Aeolus's island kingdom and collects an ox-skin bag of all winds except for the west wind, which he requires for his return voyage. In sight of home, Odysseus's greedy men tear open the bag—imagining

Double disaster: Buffeted by crosswinds, this rescue plane crashed into a truck while attempting to deliver supplies to victims of a 1976 earthquake in Guatemala.

Highly charged particles contained within this storm cloud formation deliver a shocking zap over Tucson, Arizona.

it filled with silver and gold—unleashing howling winds that blow them back to Aeolus's home.

Ancient Chinese worshipped the soil god, Yu, who harnessed rivers and tamed floods. Securing Yu's blessing was a deadly serious mission in a land where deluges along the Yangtze and Yellow Rivers have killed millions over the centuries. Gods and monsters with the power to control the forces of nature took many forms in ancient China. Weather historian Jeffrey Rosenfeld describes the stormy disaster that stopped self-appointed deity Kublai Khan dead in his tracks in 1274, when he sent a massive force of 900 ships bearing 40,000 warriors to invade Japan. The Mongol cavalry began an island-hopping campaign of terror that seemed destined to defeat the Japanese, but legend tells of a storm that destroyed more than a quarter of the khan's vessels in the harbor, forcing a retreat to the mainland. As a god himself, "Kublai Khan had good reason to believe that the failure was a fluke," Rosenfeld writes. "So he gave the weather, and his warriors, another chance. The Khan ordered whole forests cleared in China to build new fleets. They set sail from Korea and China and arrived at Hakata Bay, Kyushu, in August—the height of the typhoon season. This time history is unambiguous: on August 15, two days of ferocious rains began. Furious winds and towering waves dashed the Mongol ships to pieces; the storm-stirred surge of water into the harbor made escape impossible. More than 100,000 Mongol warriors and their sailors were killed in the storm or abandoned to certain death at the hands of the Japanese. It was said that the wreckage of ships was so dense that a person could walk across Hakata Bay after the storm. The typhoon gave birth to a legend on invincibility in Japan: a divine wind, 'kamikaze,' was said to protect its shores from invasion."

Carib Indians called violent rainstorms *huracan,* after their tempestuous god of storms and lightning. Guatemala's Quiché Maya trembled in the face of thunderstorms, believing them to be the work of the god Huracan (also known as the Heart of Sky), who represented nature at full-force frenzy. Spaniards, unfamiliar with the storms themselves, used the word *huracán* to evoke the uncontrollable forces that faced them in the New World. But the tropical cataclysm that 16th-century conquistadores found frightfully fascinating had already left its mark on New World history in dozens of important events. Christopher Columbus built the first European town on the island of Hispaniola (Haiti) on his second trip to the New World, but a hurricane quickly destroyed it. In 1500 a hurricane sank 90 gold-laden ships and drowned 500 sailors sent back to Spain by Columbus. "Eyes never beheld the seas so high, angry and covered by foam. . . .We were forced to keep out in this bloody ocean, seething like a pot on a hot fire. Never did the sky look more terrible. . . . All this time the water never ceased to fall from the sky. . . . It was like another deluge. . . . The people were so worn out that they longed for death to end their dreadful suffering," wrote the great navigator, describing a 1503 hurricane he encountered at sea near Panama. A hurricane was even responsible for blowing the *Mayflower* off course in 1620, forcing a landing in Massachusetts, instead of *Virginia.*

Extreme weather provides dramatic background in the plays of William Shakespeare. *Macbeth* opens with a violent storm and scheming witches who foretell the bloodbath that the new king will bring. "It will be rain to-night," says Banquo; his assassin responds, "Let it come down." Scholars believe that a 1609 hurricane—which tormented a British colonial fleet on its way to Jamestown, Virginia, sinking one vessel and causing another to crash on (and consequently settle) Bermuda—provided the stormy inspiration that Shakespeare turned into Prospero's magical and manipulative enticement in *The Tempest.* And in the tragedy *King Lear,* the old, mad monarch rages on a heath under a roiling storm: Blow, winds, and crack your cheeks! rage! blow! / You cataracts and hurricanoes, spout / Till you have drench'd our steeples, drown'd the cocks! / You sulphurous and thought-executing fires, / Vaunt-couriers to oak-cleaving thunderbolts, / Singe my white head! And thou, all-shaking thunder, / Smite flat the thick rotundity o' the world!

As long as winds and rains rage against the Earth, poets and artists will have plenty of inspiration. Academics and meteorologists, meanwhile, will have their work cut out for them. Weather has shaped the course of history in indelible ways. In 1588, a series of summer storms in the English Channel enabled the British Navy to defeat the Spanish Armada. But the winds of fortune blow separate ways: A summer thunderstorm helped save Washington, D.C., from total destruction during the War of 1812 by quenching fires set by the pyromaniacal, imperialist British. Modern scientific inquiry into the causes, patterns, and predictability of weather has led to astonishing and lifesaving discoveries. But a force as defining as weather sometimes seems on a scale too grand for scientific reduction. Even today, with satellites speckling the sky and ushering an endless stream of data ripe for forecasters, describing the extreme forces of weather still seems more of an art than a science. At times, when nature's raging forces threaten to overcome us, it somehow seems appropriate to imagine extreme weather as manifestations of Jupiter, who reigned over the Roman pantheon and was revered as the god of thunder and lightning and the sender of rain, or mighty Thor, god of thunder in Norse mythology, whose hammer causes thunderclaps and chariot scorches the Earth. Such is the smallness of humankind in the face of our vast natural torments.

WHAT IS WEATHER?

And yet, despite our inclination to ascribe extreme forces to mythological powers, weather can be understood scientifically. Unlike climate, which refers to average weather conditions over a period possibly of years, weather is measured in more finite increments. The American Meteorological Society defines weather as "the state of the atmosphere, mainly with respect to its effect upon life and human activities at a particular time." Or, phrased in a way iconoclastic English wit and scientific rationalist Samuel Johnson might appreciate, climate is what you expect, weather is what you get.

The energy driving the planet's weather systems and atmospheric circulation begins with the sun, which radiates heat and light onto the tilted, rotating Earth, unevenly warming our world's surface. The resulting temperature differences cause moisture-laden tropical air masses to heat, expand, and rise toward the Poles; meanwhile, polar air masses cool, contract, and sink back toward the Equator. These circulating air masses create pressure variations leading to changes in weather. The Earth's rotation further affects shifting air currents, resulting in the Coriolis Effect (named for French physics professor Gaspard-Gustave de Coriolis, who identified the effect in 1835). This effect influences the wind belts circulating between the Poles and tropical regions—the high-altitude meandering jet streams and the trade winds blowing toward the Equator.

Pressure differences and the Coriolis Effect drive the movement of air masses; the leading edges of these masses form fluctuating battle lines where warm and cold fronts meet and clash, creating high winds, temperature changes, rising or falling pressure, clouds, and storms. Landmasses, ocean temperatures and currents, and the sun's radiant energy greatly affect this dynamic system. One of the most dramatic windstorms on record partially flattened France on December 26-27, 1999. In the early morning hours, a hurricane-like weather system blew across western Europe with 130-mile per-hour winds. Within 30 hours the gusty storm had leveled more than a million acres, felled more than 270 million trees, and caused more than a hundred deaths. An infamous 1703 cyclone in Great Britain brought

Gale-force winds robbed New Yorkers of their balance as an 1888 blizzard blanketed Gotham in unprecedented plumes of snow.

winds that leveled thousands of homes, tens of thousands of trees, and hundreds of Royal Navy ships, along with some 8,000 sailors.

Each day heat from the sun evaporates trillions of tons of water from the Earth's oceans, lakes, rivers, and land; energy is then stored in water vapor until it is released during condensation as water droplets or ice crystals. Droplets or crystals that adhere to dust particles create the visible currents of air we call clouds. Warm, dry air acts like a sponge, soaking up moisture until it becomes saturated. When this heavy, water droplet–laden air sponge is cooled as it rises up to the cooler atmosphere aloft, it releases its load of water as rain or snow. Clouds are harbingers of weather to come. Scattered cumulus (Latin for "heap") clouds against a blue sky promise a fair, dry day. Massive, gray thunderheads portend high winds and precipitation. At any given moment some 1,800 thunderstorms are in progress across the globe. These events—which occur when an updraft of warm, moisture-laden air rises to clash with higher, colder air—range from single-cell storms (a convective loop of one pair of up-and-down drafts) to supercell thunderstorms, which have deep, rotating updrafts and can generate extreme weather, such as hail and tornadoes. These, in turn, can bring on flash floods and mudslides, such as those that swept 15,000 people to their death in Venezuela, following a torrential 1999 rainstorm.

Thunderstorms can even gang up into a long swath of damaging winds called *derechos*. These mini weather systems can stretch for 250 miles, generating dangerously strong winds. In 1995, in New York State, a derecho toppled millions of trees over more than a million acres, killing five campers. A similar event in Baltimore's Inner Harbor in 2004 caused a water taxi to capsize, killing 5 of the 25 people aboard.

The most illuminating thunderstorm effect is lightning, which occurs when negative electrical charges reach down from the bottom of a cloud and prompt a positive charge to rise from the ground at speeds clocked at 14,000 miles per hour. Lightning, in turn, creates thunder, by instantly heating air up to 55,000°F; the expansion and contraction of superheated air sets air molecules in movement, creating sound waves that travel at about 730 miles per hour. Around the world, lightning strikes the ground about a hundred times per second; after flash floods, lightning is the biggest weather killer in the United States, fatally zapping nearly a hundred people each year. Globally, satellite images have detected clusters of lightning activity over hot spots on land. Florida, where moist air from the Atlantic and Gulf of Mexico collides, is one high-strike zone. Central Africa, where thunderstorms occur year-round, is another. North Africa, western China, and small Pacific islands very rarely experience

"To look up to the sky for the nutriment of our bodies, is the condition of nature; to call upon the sun for peace and gaiety, or deprecate the clouds lest sorrow should overwhelm us, is the cowardice of idleness, and the idolatry of folly."

—SAMUEL JOHNSON, *IDLER*

lightning zaps. Although the chance of being hit by lightning is about one in three million, thunderbolts still get away with murder. About one in four people who are struck are killed, according to the National Oceanic and Atmospheric Administration.

Benjamin Franklin—labeled the modern Prometheus by philosopher Immanuel Kant, in honor of the Greek god who stole fire from the heavens and bestowed it on humankind—was the first to suggest that lightning was electricity, and in 1752 he bravely (some say suicidally) flew a kite into a thunderstorm and watched as sparks jumped from a key hanging on the kite string to the knuckles on his hand. Franklin's electrifying discoveries became the basis of the lightning rod. American painter Martin Johnson Heade's masterpiece "Thunder Storm on Narragansett Bay" (1868) depicts an eerie, almost surreal vision of nature's dominion over man. Heade's evocative image has been interpreted as suggestive of the rift in the American national identity following the Civil War, and thunderstorm metaphors were frequently invoked in the 19th century to describe the trials of life—individual, collective, even political. In his 1865 poem "Rise O Days from Your Fathomless Deeps," Walt Whitman wrote: "I heard the

Commuters, guided by posts, make their way home though a jifubuki, or ground blizzard, on Honshu Island, Japan.

wind piping, I saw the black clouds. . . . / Heard the continuous thunder as it bellowed after the lightning. . . . / How Democracy with desperate vengeful port strides on, shown through the dark by those flashes of lightning! . . . / Thunder on! stride on, Democracy! strike with vengeful stroke!" But this optimistic song is of little assurance to the residents of Kampala, Uganda, who endure a thunderstorm 290 days a year, on average. Or to Warwick Marks, an Australian farmer, who lost 68 cows when lightning struck the tree sheltering them (the electric charge spread out into the surrounding soil) on October 31, 2005.

A frosty and more deadly manifestation of violent weather produces snowstorms, quick onslaughts of heavy snow, ice accumulation, and dangerous wind chills. The cold alone can be murderous: Among the iciest temperatures recorded in North America was a 1947 reading of -81.4°F in Canada's Yukon. "We threw a dish of water high into the air, just to see what would happen," one frigid observer is quoted in *Extreme Weather.* "Before it hit the ground, it made a hissing noise, froze, and fell as tiny round pellets of ice the size of wheat kernels. Metal snapped like ice; wood became petrified; and rubber was just like cement. Patches of human breath fog remained in the still air for three or four minutes before fading away."

Falling snow accompanied by winds of more than 35 miles per hour produces blizzards. One of the most destructive winter events was the Superstorm of 1993, a massive cyclonic storm that raged in mid-March along the East Coast of North America, affecting more than 26 states and eastern Canada. Hurricane-force winds in Cuba and Florida produced Gulf Coast storm surges and tornadoes that killed dozens of people. The storm is best remembered for the fierce blizzard that blanketed snow across areas as far south as Florida. Among the murderous forces that killed 270 people and affected more than 100 million were deep freezes, hurricane-force winds, crashing waves, twisters, and sleet.

The Superstorm recalled for some historians the Great Blizzard of 1899, in which a severe cold wave delivered subzero temperatures to every part of the East Coast from Tallahassee (-2°F) to Maine. For comparable kill rates, historians look to the Great Blizzard of 1888, the "Great White Hurricane," one of the most severe blizzards in American history, which paralyzed the East Coast with snow walls up to 50 inches high and 45-mile-per-hour gusts of wind that created drifts of 40 to 50 feet. One hundred people were killed in New York City alone and an estimated 400 people died from the storm overall. Other killer blizzards include the New England Blizzard of 1978 (54 deaths) and a 1996 blitz, which dropped 20 inches of snow on Manhattan and caused 200 deaths. But even this white catastrophe pales in comparison to the Iran Blizzard of 1972. The tremendous snowfalls ended a four-year drought, but the week-long cold and impassable drifts caused the death of approximately 4,000 people.

The earliest known photograph of a tornado freezes in time the ferocity of a twister that blazed a trail 22 miles southwest of Howard, South Dakota, on August 28, 1884. North America's deadly Tornado Alley appears as a patchwork of calamity in this map of the frequency of twisters with intensities of F3, F4, and F5.

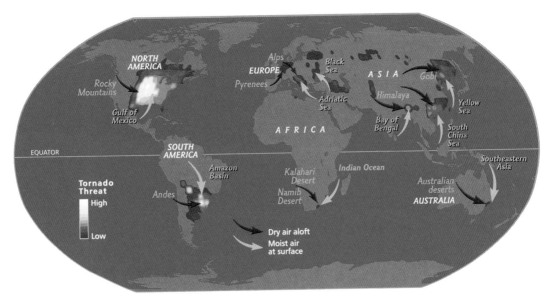

TWISTED LOGIC

"[T]ornadoes remain the black holes of meteorology," says Priit Vesilind in *National Geographic*. "Exactly how and why they form, and what drives their terrible power, are only partially understood." The simplest understanding of twisters is that they occur when strong winds flow over weaker winds, causing the air between them to spin on a horizontal axis, like a pencil rolling on a table. When a vigorous updraft interacts with the spinning air, its rotation forms a rotating wall cloud. This rotating air can be dragged by a downdraft toward the ground, where it forms into a funnel that spins down to Earth powered by the fury of 300-mile-per-hour winds. These deadly twisters, nature's most violent storms, can destroy everything in their unpredictable path. The Fujita scale, which classifies twisters according to the damage they cause, ranges from F0 ("light" or "gale") to F6 ("inconceivable"), passing "severe," "devastating," and "incredible" along the way.

More than a thousand tornadoes touch down each year in the United States, particularly east of the Rocky Mountains, in Texas, Oklahoma, Kansas, and Missouri—states in a swath notoriously known as Tornado Alley. On April 3-4, 1974, 148 tornadoes swept across 13 states in this belt, setting a twisted twister record. After 16 cyclonic hours, 330 people were dead and 5,484 others were injured, according to NOAA. At the peak of this Super Outbreak, 15 funnels were on the ground at the same time. In 2005, a series of tornadoes rampaged across a 41-mile front in Indiana and Kentucky, killing 23 people and leaving 200 injured. In 2006, a tornado hit a mobile home park in North Carolina, killing seven people. Although this event pales in comparison with the 1984 outbreak of 22 twisters that killed 57 people in the Carolinas, it reinforces the persistent fury of funnel power. The Tri-State Tornado of March 18, 1925, ranks as the deadliest U.S. twister. In a spree that cut a 219-mile path of destruction through Missouri, Illinois, and Indiana, this violent vortex killed 689 people; in Murphysboro, Illinois, alone, the tornado claimed 234 lives. The

The 15 Deadliest U.S. Tornadoes

Location	Date	Death Toll
Missouri/Illinois/Indiana	March 18, 1925	695
Natchez, Mississippi	May 6, 1840	317
St. Louis, Missouri	May 27, 1896	255
Tupelo, Mississippi	April 5, 1936	216
Gainseville, Georgia	April 6, 1936	203
Woodward, Oklahoma	April 9, 1947	181
Amite, Louisiana/ Purvis, Mississippi	April 24, 1908	143
New Richmond, Wisconsin	June 12, 1899	117
Flint, Michigan	June 8, 1953	115
Waco, Texas	May 11, 1953	114
Goliad, Texas	May 18, 1902	114
Omaha, Nebraska	March 23, 1913	103
Mattoon, Illinois	May 26, 1917	101
Shinnston, West Virginia	June 23, 1944	100
Marshfield, Missouri	April 18, 1880	99

Source: Storm Prediction Center, National Oceanic and Atmospheric Administration

This bird's-eye view of a wrecked neighborhood in Osceola County, Florida, reveals a tornado's violent path.

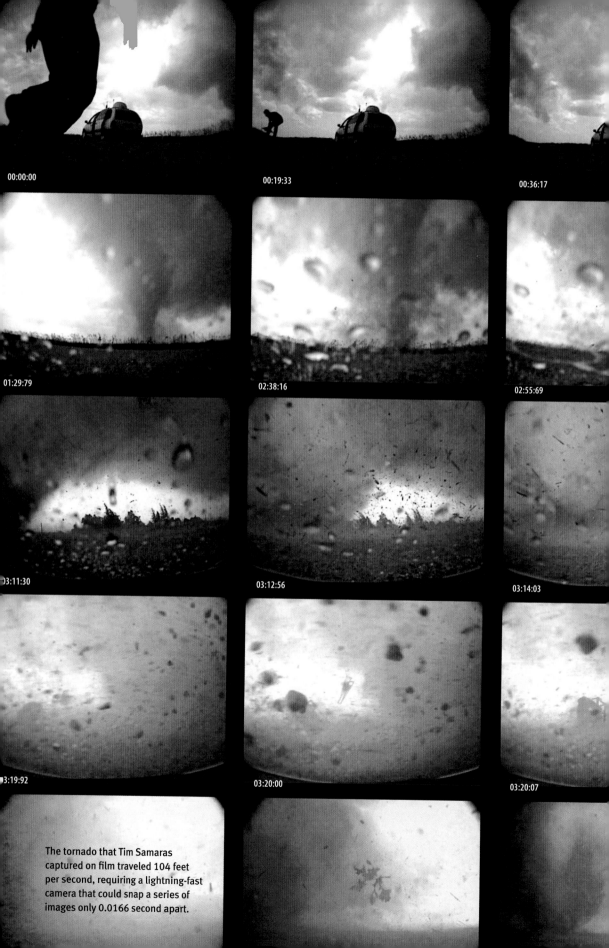

00:00:00

00:19:33

00:36:17

01:29:79

02:38:16

02:55:69

03:11:30

03:12:56

03:14:03

03:19:92

03:20:00

03:20:07

The tornado that Tim Samaras
captured on film traveled 104 feet
per second, requiring a lightning-fast
camera that could snap a series of
images only 0.0166 second apart.

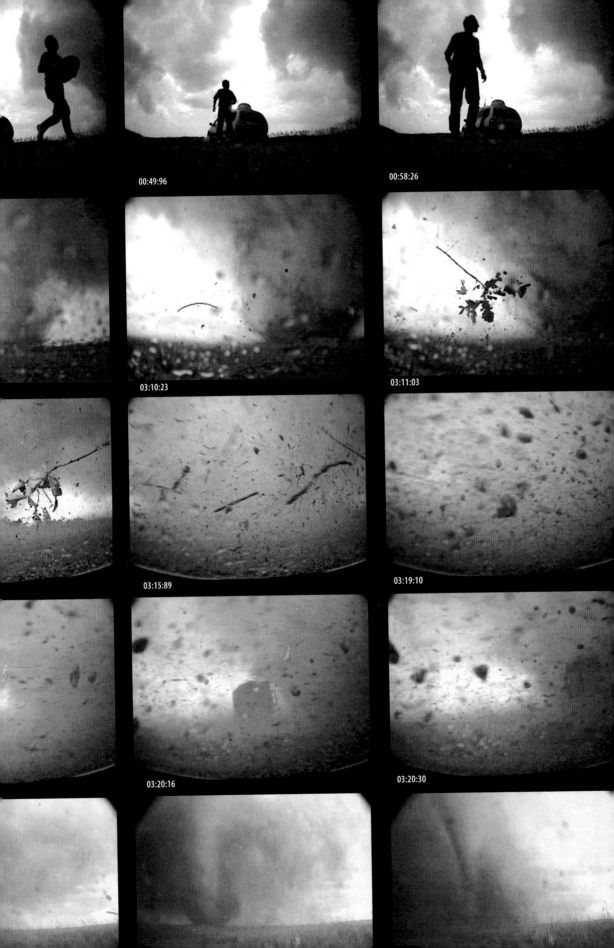

" That's the closest I've been to a violent tornado, and I have no desire to ever be that close again. The rumble rattled the whole countryside, like a waterfall powered by a jet engine. Debris was flying overhead, telephone poles were snapped and flung 300 yards through the air, roads ripped from the ground, and the town of Manchester literally sucked into the clouds. You could see the tornado's path perfectly carved through a cornfield where, like a giant harvester, it had mowed stalks down to the ground."

— TIM SAMARAS, TORNADO CHASER

deadliest twister in world history was the Daultipur-Salturia, Bangladesh Tornado, which killed approximately 1,300 people in 1989.

Engineer and tornado chaser Tim Samaras, with the help of his pyramid-shaped probes, is the first scientist to achieve measurements of humidity, temperature, pressure, wind speed, and direction in the vortex of a twister.

Samaras spends each springtime in a van outfitted with GPS, radios, scanners, monitors, a wireless Internet connection, and satellite tracking instruments, hoping to spot tornadoes and deploy computer-crammed probes in their path. In 2003, on a sleepy country road near Manchester, South Dakota, a half-mile-wide tornado barreled across the landscape with more than 200-mile-an-hour winds. Samaras deployed three probes, 60 seconds before a tornado crossed the exact spot at full force. The probes survived to reveal the biggest drop in barometric pressure ever recorded—equivalent to stepping into an elevator and hurtling up 1,000 feet in ten seconds. A year after that achievement, Samaras did the near impossible: He chased down a tornado and placed a probe with video cameras directly in its path. The powerful twister passed ten feet from the probe, giving the cameras the first-ever video images inside a tornado. This close encounter made it possible for Samaras to calculate wind speeds closer to the ground than ever before.

"Data from the probes helps us understand tornado dynamics and how they form. With that piece of the puzzle we can make more precise forecasts and ultimately give people earlier warnings," explains Samaras, whose brave, if twisted, preoccupation came at an early age. "It all started when I was about six years old and saw that fantastic tornado in *The Wizard of Oz.*"

EYE OF THE STORM

Killer hurricanes spell gloom and doom whether they are called typhoons in the western Pacific or tropical cyclones in the Indian Ocean. These circulating weather systems can jet themselves to an altitude of tens of thousands of feet, where rising air finally vents in a spiraling exhaust of cirrus clouds. One of the great meteorological mysteries is why some tropical depressions (a cluster of thunderstorms that coalesces into a weather system under low atmospheric pressure) become hurricanes and others become mere tropical storms. The answer to this mystery seems to lie in a perfectly sinister mixture of low pressure, moist air, warm water, and little wind shear. Hurricanes form when a cluster of thunderstorms gathers to create a low-pressure area that draws in and generates spin in a counterclockwise direction. Fueled by the heat of sun-drenched tropical seas that send warm, moist air into the frigid upper atmosphere, and unmitigated by strong winds that break up the storm, this swirling devil becomes a hurricane when its winds surpass 74 miles per hour and a telltale "eye" forms in its center. This eye looks into the heart of a deadly sky.

Retired NOAA P-3 "Hurricane Hunter" Cmdr. Ron Philippsborn describes what it is like to fly through a hurricane:

We hit the eyewall. The winds climb rapidly, 90, 110, 125 knots, howling at the airplane from the left side, and the plane starts to buck. . . . Wind shears hammer the P-3 up and down; the rain is like a fire hose blasting the windows. The plane shakes so violently that the numbers on the instrument panel are unreadable. . . . One last updraft on the inner edge of the eyewall slams into the belly of the plane. Suddenly all is calm. We're through the eyewall and into the eye, and the view is breathtaking. The surrounding wall of clouds, beautiful, menacing and awe-inspiring . . . looms tens of thousands of feet into the sky, encircling us, gently curving outward in a "stadium effect." Above us, clear blue sky; below, an angry sea whipped into a frenzy by howling winds.

A thunderstorm lasting several hours generates energy equivalent to that of a small hydrogen bomb, whereas a hurricane releases an equivalent amount of energy every second. Even an average hurricane packs some 1.5 trillion watts of power in its

A storm's fury is all too often only the initial catastrophe in a weather-wracked region. A massive storm, such as the 1970 Bhola cyclone in Bangladesh, has the power to unleash an unending cascade of sorrow that can include flooding, looting, water shortages, famine, and disease. This mother and daughter, photographed in a refugee camp, barely survived the Bangladesh cyclone and were forced to confront life in a world utterly changed by the disaster.

winds—equivalent to about half the world's entire electrical generating capacity. Hurricane force is measured by the Saffir-Simpson scale, developed in the 1960s and 1970s to quantify potential wind damage and storm-surge heights. The basic five-point scale measures four factors: barometric pressure, wind speed, storm surge, and damage potential. A minimal Category 1 storm will produce 74- to 95-mile-per-hour sustained winds and bring a storm surge of four to five feet. An extreme Category 3 event has sustained winds that clock at 111 to 130 miles per hour and a 9- to 12-foot surge. Catastrophic Category 5 hurricanes bring winds

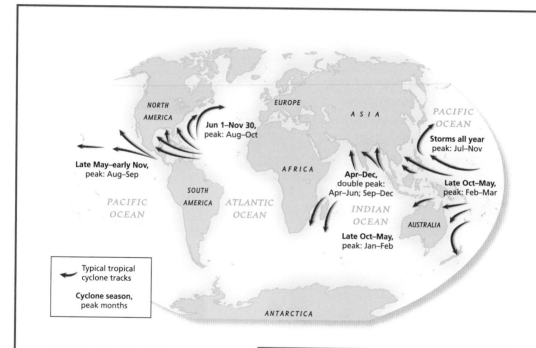

Tropical cyclones (and their counterparts hurricanes and typhoons) develop in warm bodies of water near the Equator during the warmer months and follow the prevailing wind currents.

Deadly Typhoons Cyclones, and Hurricanes

Event/Location	Death Toll	Year
Cyclone/Bangladesh	300,000-500,000	1970
Cyclone/Bangladesh	138,000+	1991
Typhoon/China	60,000	1922
Typhoon/China	50,000	1912
Hurricane/U.S.	11,000	1998
Typhoon/Philippines	6,000	1991
Typhoon/Japan	5,000	1959

Source: National Oceanic and Atmospheric Administration

that exceed 155 miles per hour and a storm surge of 18 feet or more. The measurement of a storm surge is essential, for as devastating as 130-mile-per-hour winds can be, it is often the overwhelming walls of water—which rise due to the extremely low atmospheric pressure beneath the storm that in effect pulls up the very surface of the ocean—that are a cyclone's death sentence.

Water, not wind, was Katrina's primary agent of destruction. The storm surge pushed in front of Katrina rose some 20 feet, even though the storm had reduced in ferocity from Category 5 to a landfall force of Category 3. Had the hurricane landed with full force, New Orleans might well have been washed off the map. Instead, it was the relentless surge of water that stormed over barrier islands and wetland buffer zones to crash levees, inundate lakes, and thrash protective barriers. Katrina, with 1,836 deaths, was the third deadliest hurricane in U.S. history. The superstorm left washed-out stretches along the Gulf Coast, with the once lush shores of Louisiana, Mississippi, and Alabama reduced to scrap heaps of splintered wood, tattered plastic, concrete shards, and metal debris. With tragic consequences, 2005 was a year of cyclonic superlatives: Never before had a hurricane caused as much economic damage as Katrina. Never before had the Atlantic seen 27 named tropical storms, 7 of which made U.S. landfall. Never before had 15 hurricanes been spotted in a single season, including four Category 5 storms.

The largest hurricane ever, the 1979 Pacific typhoon Tip, sent gale-force winds across more than 650 miles. But the most memorable cyclones are measured not in terms of scale or storm surge, but in lives lost. The storm that leveled the island city of Galveston, Texas, in 1900 was a tropical terror that left between 8,000 and 12,000 dead—perhaps one quarter of the city's total population. Not a single building escaped damage from the storm, which swept away 3,000 homes and left thousands without shelter. "With a raging sea rolling around them, with a wind so terrific that none could hope to escape its fury, with roofs being torn away and buildings crumbling," reported one survivor of the deadliest natural disaster in U.S. history, which killed more Americans than the Great Chicago Fire of 1871, the 1906 San Francisco earthquake, and the 1889 Johnstown, Pennsylvania, flood combined. Galveston residents "huddled like rats in the structures. As buildings crumpled and crashed, hundreds were buried under the debris, while thousands were thrown into the waters, some to meet instant death, others to struggle for a time in vain, and yet other thousands to escape death in miraculous and marvelous ways." Survivors emerged from their stupor to find bodies stripped bare by flying nails, broken glass, and jagged wood clogging Galveston Bay, along with the corpses of cows, horses, and dogs. Hot weather after the storm turned the city into one of funeral pyres; dark clouds lingered over the island for weeks, and a pall for decades.

Kamikazes, those divine winds of myth, have spun an unending coil of real-life misery from ancient times to today. Their names connote more than historic waves of death and destruction—they call to mind the immediate terror of natural disaster. The 1928 hurricane that roared across Florida, pushing a wall of water through several small lakeside towns and overflowing Lake Okeechobee, where 1,836 drowned, is known by one name: Okeechobee. In 1969, Camille pursued a deadly trajectory, bolstered by 210-mile-per-hour winds and a 25-foot-high storm surge, uprooting and killing at a frenetic pace along the Gulf Coast. Andrew ravaged a swath of southern Florida and Louisiana in 1992, leaving behind an estimated $26.5 billion in damages. Mitch was responsible for the death of between 11,000 and 18,000 Hondurans and Nicaraguans in 1998. Frances was one of four calamitous cyclones to smack Florida's Gulf coast in 2004, followed by Ivan and Jeanne. More than 3,000 people died in Haiti when Jeanne unleashed mudslides, a few weeks after Charley brought woe to Cubans.

The deadliest Atlantic hurricane in history was the Great Hurricane of 1780, which swept across the Caribbean, nearly wiping out the British fleet and killing some 22,000 sailors and townspeople on a number of islands. But the world's most intense tropical storms have all been western Pacific typhoons, fomented in a region that is home to the strongest and most frequent tropical storms. Polynesia, Taiwan, Korea, and Japan are frequently visited by typhoons. A furious 1828 cyclone submerged parts of the city of Nagasaki, drowning an estimated 15,000 people. As ghastly as that death tally may be, the bloody Bay of Bengal holds history's record for the deadliest tropical storms. Densely populated, low-lying coastal communities here suffered the brunt of the deadliest tropical storm in recorded history. In November 1970, the Bhola cyclone ripped over the Brahmaputra River Delta of Bangladesh, sending a 30-foot storm surge over crowded offshore islands. Flooding and related horrors killed about half a million people, making it the deadliest hurricane ever. Another deadly cyclone struck the delta regions of Bangladesh in 1991, killing more than 138,000 people. The tropical cyclone devastated the coastal area southeast of Dhaka with a 20-foot storm surge.

One of the few grace notes to emerge from the 1970 Bangladesh catastrophe came via song. In response to the deafening tragedy and its long-term dissonance, former Beatle George Harrison organized the Concert for Bangladesh, the first benefit concert of its magnitude in world history. This 1971 concert, headlined by Bob Dylan, Ravi Shankar, and others, raised $243,418.50 for Bangladesh relief. "Bangladesh, Bangladesh / Where so many people are dying fast / And it sure looks like a mess / I've never seen such distress / Now won't you lend your hand and try to understand / Relieve the people of Bangladesh," sang Harrison, ushering in an era of star-studded humanitarian approaches to natural

A newspaper's plaintive headline speaks volumes for Mary Mason, stranded at a rescue shelter in Biloxi, Mississippi, after being left homeless by Hurricane Katrina in 2005. Thousands of others shared Mason's grief and uncertainty. More than a year after the catastrophic storm, countless survivors were left scattered across the nation with little hope for timely resettlement. The underlying rain structure of Hurricane Katrina, on Sunday, August 28, at 10:25 p.m., is revealed in this graphic based on information gathered by precipitation radar, visible infrared scanner, and tropical microwave imager. Blue represents areas with at least 0.25 inch of rain per hour, green shows at least 0.5 inch, yellow represents 1 inch, and red signifies at least 2 inches.

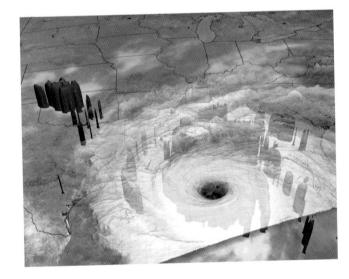

Rescuers in Guayama, Puerto Rico, struggle to keep a young child from being swept away by flood waters caused by Hurricane Hortense in 1996.

disaster, including the 1985 Live Aid concerts, whose proceeds went to famine-ridden Ethiopia, and events that generated millions of dollars for those affected by the 2004 Southeast Asian tsunami and Hurricane Katrina. Benefit concerts help survivors in catastrophe's aftermath, but they can do little to reduce the wrath of raging forces. Cyclones heed no call for mercy. In November 2006, Typhoon Durian battered the Philippines, triggering deadly mudslides that killed more than 700 people, displaced more than 95,000, and left 3 million without food, electricity, or water. Durian struck at the foot of Mayon, the Philippines' most active volcano, which had been threatening full-bore eruption for months. In an instant, landscapes liquefy and lives are lost across our ever changing planet.

WATERY GRAVES

As with the tides of Katrina and the torrents of Bangladesh, water, not howling winds, brought death to the masses. Neither as dramatic as hurricanes nor as vivid as tornadoes, floods are the most frequent and lethal of all natural disasters. Frequent because our planet is a watery one, with more than 70 percent of its surface covered with water and more than 97 percent of that water locked in oceans—enough to create a two-mile-deep pool around the globe, if spread evenly—fueling an endless water cycle of evaporation and precipitation. And lethal because more than half the world's population lives on sea coasts, in river deltas, or along estuaries and river mouths. Even populations in typically parched areas are not immune from floods. In 2006, East Africa's most severe flood season in half a century plunged the breadbaskets of Somalia and Ethiopia underwater, creating the conditions for an extended famine in an impoverished area already strafed by anarchy and war. In short order the floods left hundreds dead by drowning, starvation, water-borne diseases like cholera and malaria, and even crocodile attacks, as rising waters brought the heartless reptiles ever closer to villages.

As the biblical deluge that Noah and his animals survived in an ark suggests, flooding has been around forever. But the world's most persistently waterlogged places, such as Mount Waialeale on the Hawaiian island of Kauai and Mawsynram and Cherrapunji, in Assam, India (all of which receive, on average, more than 460 inches of rain each year), are not where the world's deadliest floods

Top Ten Floods of the 20th Century

Country	Year	Deaths
China	1931	3.7 million
China	1959	2 million
China	1939	500,000
China	1935	142,000
China	1911	100,000
China	1949	57,000
Guatemala	1949	40,000
China	1954	30,000
Venezuela	1999	30,000
Bangladesh	1974	28,700

Source: EM-DAT: The OFDA/CRED International Disaster Database (www.em-dat.net), Université Catholique de Louvain, Brussels, Belgium

Fetid water inundated the Verdot family's trailer in Taos, Missouri, after the Mississippi River Flood of 1993.

have taken place. In fact, less than a quarter of all rainfall has the potential to become floodwater. Rather it is geography and human efforts at irrigation that determine the direction and impact of floodwaters. Ancient Egyptians famously succeeded in taming the Nile, but ancient and modern Chinese have failed catastrophically to manage severe flooding associated with heavy rainfall along the Yellow (Huang) and Yangtze Rivers. These monstrous rivers, which have sustained Chinese civilization across the ages, have also violently resisted efforts to control them, from earthen dikes to modern dams. For good reason is the silt-filled, flood-prone Yellow River commonly known as China's Sorrow. And yet it is the murderous Yangtze, the longest river in Asia and the third longest in the world (after the Nile and the Amazon), that tallies its death toll in the millions. In the past 2,000 years, the Yangtze has flooded more than a thousand times.

Born in the mountains of Tibet, the Yangtze is fed by some 700 major tributaries as it swirls through China's heartland, buffered by plains that support a third of the nation's population. An ancient and failing system of levees, intended to protect against inundation, is now giving way to the monumental Three Gorges Dam project, but the floods that have wreaked havoc since ancient times remain a persistent threat. In 1931, powerful thunderstorms sent water raging over the Yangtze's battlements. This event was history's most severe flood; it affected more than 51 million people and left a possible 3.7 million dead from drowning, disease, and starvation.

Few places are immune from flooding, and even modern dam technology will not always save the day. The Midwest's Great Flood of 1993, fueled by heavy winter snowfall and persistent spring and summer rains, inundated the Mississippi's upper section, flooding farms and cities adjacent to the river in Iowa and Missouri, causing 50 deaths and billions of dollars in damage. The Mississippi, North America's second longest river, runs some 2,400 miles and is fed by an estimated 100,000 streams and four major rivers. This mighty river has consistently mocked attempts to control its flow—reservoirs, spillways, barrages, cutoffs, levees, and revetments—that unimpressed river men dismiss out of hand. "One who knows the Mississippi will promptly aver—not aloud but to himself—that ten thousand River Commissions, with the mines of the world at their back, cannot tame that lawless stream, cannot curb it or confine it, cannot say to it, 'Go here,' or 'Go there,' and make it obey," wrote Mark Twain in *Life on the Mississippi.*

Not quite 50 years later, the Great Mississippi Flood of 1927 proved Twain's words to be harrowingly prescient. This catastrophic inundation forced more than 700,000 people to abandon their homes when the mighty river broke through dozens of hastily built levees and unleashed floodwaters across 27,000 square miles of land, leaving at least 246 people dead in seven states. Between one and two feet of rain deluged states from Illinois to Louisiana, and the worst of the flooding occurred upriver from New Orleans. The drenching event led to the federal flood-control program and gave the Army Corps of Engineers the job of controlling the nation's rivers. Locals displaced by the flood wondered if they would ever return home—and many didn't.

Each year more than a hundred Americans die due to floods, as many thousands more perish around the world. Flash floods—prompted by fast and heavy precipitation or a dam failure—are the deadliest and least predictable of all deluges, and they can strike nearly anywhere in the world. In 1889, one of America's most morbidly memorable floods claimed some 2,200 lives around Johnstown, Pennsylvania, when the decaying South Fork Dam, built to hold back the waters of a high-ground lake, gave way, sending a cascade roaring down the narrow Conemaugh River valley. The worst dam burst in U.S. history sent a water wall 35 feet high, swamping the village of South Fork and towns downstream. "It seemed as if a forest was coming down upon us. There was a great wall of water roaring and gliding swiftly along, so thickly studded with the trees . . . that it looked like a gigantic avalanche," recalled one fortunate survivor of the disaster. Less lucky was Anna Fenn, who lost seven children and her husband in the flood-driven water, mud, and rocks. "The water rose and floated us until our heads nearly touched the ceiling," she wrote. "The air was stifling, and I could not tell just the moment the rest of the children had to give up and drown . . . what I suffered, with the bodies of seven children floating around me in the gloom, can never be told." ■

Burning houses are swept down the swollen Conemaugh River and locals perish as the waters of the 1889 Johnstown Flood bring death to a Pennsylvania town.

Swarms of pink locusts descended in 2004 on the Giza Pyramids near Cairo, Egypt.

IMPENDING DOOM

CHAPTER 6

Impending Doom: Climate and Humanity

> "Now the wind grew strong and hard and it worked at the rain crust in the corn fields. Little by little the sky was darkened by the mixing dust, and the wind felt over the earth, loosened the dust and carried it away."
>
> —JOHN STEINBECK, *THE GRAPES OF WRATH*

Black blizzards make for a sinister counterpoint to the white death brought on by snowstorms. The unstoppable dirt winds that ripped through the Great Plains during the 1930s Dust Bowl left an indelible mark not just on the land—where millions of tons of parched topsoil were swept up into towering "dusters" that brought darkness at noon—but on the Americans affected by this brutally prolonged drought. Spring and summer rains repeatedly failed, shriveling crops in once fertile fields that formed the nation's breadbasket. Malnourished cows stopped producing milk; rivers chalked up; and the desiccated land, barren of vegetation, succumbed to the relentless gusts, which became like curtains of dust. "The wind grew stronger. The rain crust broke and the dust lifted up out of the fields and drove gray plumes into the air like sluggish smoke. The corn threshed the wind and made a dry, rushing sound. The finest dust did not settle back to earth now, but disappeared into the darkening sky," wrote John Steinbeck in *The Grapes of Wrath*, which describes the plight of farm families (Okies—refugees from Oklahoma, Texas, Kansas, Arkansas, and Missouri) uprooted, financially ruined, and turned into wandering paupers by the merciless drought.

The dust storm known as Black Sunday came on April 14, 1935, and in a single day swept up 300,000 tons of topsoil—twice as much dirt as was dug out of the Panama Canal during seven years of construction—that choked people and blanketed houses across five midwestern states, from the Dakotas to Texas. Static electricity created by the dust clung to the pitch-black air. All told, 27 states were severely affected by the drought, which covered more than three-fourths of the nation and lasted for the better part of a decade. An

Ben Shahn's 1936 poster for the U.S. government's Resettlement Administration conveys the personal toll taken by the decade's dust storms.

estimated 34 million acres of cultivated land had been rendered useless and 100 million acres had lost all or most of its topsoil to roiling dust storms by the time rains finally came in the fall of 1939, ending the eight-and-a-half-year drought that left half a million Americans homeless. "A dust storm hit, an' it hit like thunder; / It dusted us over, an' it covered us under; / Blocked out the traffic an' blocked out the sun, / Straight for home all the people did run," sang Woody Guthrie in "So Long, It's Been Good to Know Yuh." But the Dust Bowl catastrophe was not merely the result of severe drought. This disaster was fueled by decades of inappropriate agricultural practices, as farmers cleared trees and plowed under grasses that had protected the fragile topsoil from restless winds. Greed for high-value returns on crops drove the plunder of the Plains' natural vegetation. The Soil Conservation Service in Washington, D.C., formulated agricultural techniques that greatly reduced the amount of blowing earth. But the damage wrought by the longest drought in U.S. history was done.

One positive movement, however, emerged from this unmitigated disaster. Perhaps for the first time, Americans collectively realized the ecological limits of their land and the necessity for its vigilant stewardship through responsible farming and land-use practices. "The nation that destroys its soil destroys itself," wrote Franklin D. Roosevelt to state governors in 1937. The challenge of turning this awareness into action is ongoing, but the plagues of drought and desertification—heightened by the forces of global warming—make conservation in all forms an imperative. "The relationship between human civilization and the ecological system of the Earth has been utterly transformed by a combination of factors, including the population explosion, the technological revolution, and the willingness to ignore the future consequences of our present actions," writes Al Gore in *An Inconvenient Truth*. "The underlying reality is that we are colliding with the planet's ecological system, and its most vulnerable components are crumbling as a result. . . . In every corner of the globe—on land and in water, in melting ice and disappearing snow, during heat waves and droughts, in the eyes of hurricanes and in the tears of refugees—the world is witnessing mounting and undeniable evidence that nature's cycles are profoundly changing. . . . Not only does human-caused global warming exist, but it is also growing more and more dangerous, and at a pace that has now made it a planetary emergency."

THE LONG AND DUSTY ROAD

The dirty thirties were far from history's first—or last—brush with dust. Drought is a slow-motion killer, one that strangles rather than erupts. Ocean currents and jet streams cause these periodic, prolonged absences of water, which can grip a region, draining life from fields and people, and herald the onset of famine, disease, wildfires, desertification, and even war. Roughly 10 percent of the North

Dark clouds of airborne dust threaten to envelop and smother a Stratford, Texas, farm in 1935.

American continent experiences drought in any given year; the worst, a vicious 1988 drought, left Yellowstone ablaze and caused nearly 10,000 heat-related deaths. In 2006, Australia, already the Earth's most arid continent, experienced its most severe drought in hundreds of years; large swaths of western Australia, suffering from years of deficient rainfall, were forced to comply with heavy restrictions on water usage. In the same year, China's Sichuan Province experienced its worst drought in modern history, with nearly eight million people and more than seven million cattle facing water shortages. In 2005, a food crisis erupted in the African nation of Niger, following insufficient rainfall that resulted in poor harvests and dry pastures, as well as swarms of desert locust that devoured nearly all crops the year before. More than two million people were left vulnerable to food and water shortages. A widespread food shortage in the Darfur region of Sudan caused by drought has become a humanitarian crisis driven by genocidal warring factions. In many cases, political instability and resource mismanagement—not the precipitating drought—leads to the disruption of food supply and famine.

Periodic droughts plague Africa's Sahel, a broad, 3,000-mile-long stretch of semiarid grassland on the southern edge of the Sahara. This vast region includes Mauritania, Senegal, Mali, Burkina Faso, Niger, northern Nigeria, Chad, southern

Sudan, and much of Ethiopia. A severe drought-induced famine across this zone claimed more than 600,000 lives, left millions homeless, and decimated farmlands between 1968 and the mid-1980s. As in the Dust Bowl, irresponsible farming practices were partly to blame for the widespread devastation, though rising temperatures in the waters of the Indian Ocean may have contributed to the disaster. Ethiopia was gripped by droughts in the 1970s and 1980s, which became a fullbore catastrophe in 1984, when more than a million people died as a result of famine and neglect by their government. This disaster became a touchstone cultural event when a constellation of rock stars joined at the 1985 Live Aid benefit concert to raise hundreds of millions of dollars for famine relief.

Twentieth-century droughts in India, the Soviet Union, and China claimed the lives of millions, and climatologists warn that global warming may result in more extensive drought in future decades. A reflection on past human societies that have

A desolate landscape of cracked earth reflects the hardships of poor, rural Sudanese communities.

succumbed to climate swings is frightening preparation for the catastrophes to come. Well-irrigated civilizations that thrived in the Mediterranean, Egypt, and West Asia and peaked economically in 2300 B.C. subsequently withered as a result of droughts and cooling temperatures. Similarly, a farming civilization that relied on canals dried up as a result of a two-century-long drought 3,400 years ago. The Indus Valley cultures of the Harappa and the Mohenjo Daro peoples, as well as West Africa's Mali empire, were felled by drought, a blight that strikes at more people than any other natural disaster.

Researchers believe that a long period of dry climate, punctuated by three intense droughts, led to the collapse of the Maya civilization, which ranged from Mexico's Yucatán Peninsula to Honduras and peaked around A.D. 800. In a blink of time, relatively speaking, this civilization of about 15 million—who had built magnificent cities and pyramids—disappeared, leaving no clues as to the

"When the well's dry, we know the worth of water."
—BENJAMIN FRANKLIN, *POOR RICHARD'S ALMANACK*

mystery of how such a great civilization could collapse so suddenly. A similar fate befell the cliff-dwelling Anasazi tribes of the American Southwest, when drought sparked a chain of events that led to their demise. Although other factors often play a role in a civilization's collapse, including overpopulation, political instability, and weak economies, intense climatic catastrophes can provide the tipping point. As Percy Bysshe Shelley concludes in "Ozymandias of Egypt," his 1818 poem that presents the achievement of humankind as ravaged by the tyranny of time, "Two vast and trunkless legs of stone / Stand in the desert. . . . / And on the pedestal these words appear: / 'My name is Ozymandias, king of kings: / Look on my works, ye mighty, and despair!' / Nothing beside remains: round the decay / Of that colossal wreck, boundless and bare, / The lone and level sands stretch far away."

Creeping sands, such as those that threatened to bury the once mighty Ozymandias, are dangerous harbingers of the threat posed by desertification to the large fertile regions around the globe. Overpopulation forces millions of farmers onto marginal lands; growing herds of livestock overgraze the vegetation; people strip the land of trees for firewood. Whatever else remains frequently just blows away. Desertification is the creation of desertlike conditions where none existed in the recent past. Morocco, Tunisia, and Libya each loses some 250,000 acres of productive land a year to the desert. In the ever shifting sands of time, such climate change has transformed millions of square miles of vegetation to desert, but, surprisingly, the opposite is also true. Rock paintings in Algeria that date to 5000 B.C. or earlier indicate that the Sahara has experienced more rainfall in the past. Radar imagery of the Western Desert, near the boundary of modern-day Egypt and Sudan, reveals deep river valleys crossed the landscape some 35 million years ago.

Whereas in ancient times desertification depended on the interplay between climate and the land, in the past few thousand years, that interplay has expanded to include human activity. Where soil impoverishment once took place over millennia, today's degraded landscapes can take only a decade to form. "Our land, compared with what it was, is like a skeleton of a body wasted by disease," noted Plato on the deforestation of Attica in the fourth century B.C. His perception should well have been heeded in the 1960s, when water diversions from rivers feeding Asia's Aral Sea dramatically began to drain the world's fourth largest inland sea. The volume of this landlocked, polluted body of water between Kazakhstan and Uzbekistan has shrunk to less than a quarter of its original size. The World Bank and the government of Kazakhstan are working to save the sea and the communities it supports by constructing a dam on the northern part of the sea.

A grid of fencing fails to slow the advance of migrating sand dunes into an ancient Saharan oasis in Tekenket, Mauritania.

WINDS OF CHANGE

From what we know about our planet's dramatic climatic rampages, it seems only natural to feel powerless in the face of such raging forces. But there is an important distinction between the weather—a chaotic and dynamic system with immediate impact—and climate, which is the more stable and predictable average of weather when measured over time. One of the crucial differences between the two is that even as humans are forced into a passive role by the tempests of weather, they can become active participants in the variability of climate. This is because the system incorporates not just temperature, precipitation, ocean currents, and geological activity, but human factors such as agricultural, industrial, and land-use activities. The climate, in turn, affects almost everything we do in life, including the foods we eat, the places we live, and how we interact with one another.

Passionate conversations on climate and global warming are so closely identified with recent events like Hurricane Katrina that we frequently overlook ancient perspectives on climate, such as Aristotle's *Meteorologica,* written about 350 B.C. Although many of the Greek philosopher's theories on earthquakes, water evaporation, and weather phenomena—such as his theory of lightning: "When there is a great quantity of exhalation and it is rare and is squeezed out in the cloud itself we get a thunderbolt"—were later discredited, his text on earth

Stoked and scattered by hot, dry Santa Ana winds, intense 1993 fires turned parts of southern California into towering infernos.

Fiery Fates

Raging fires, which turn stretches of forest and patches of suburb into uncontrollable infernos, are stoked by drought, sparked by lightning, and whipped up by winds. When the Santa Ana sweeps westward over deserts and mountains and blows across southern California, it heats and

A California Department of Forestry employee is silhouetted in front of the flames of a burning house in the town of Paradise.

dries everything in its path, threatening to spark into flame and race across the chaparral-covered hillsides. More than half of California is covered with wildlands, where fire is a natural part of the ecological balance. As populations edge ever closer to these wild spaces, they encroach on raging forces that heed no human-made boundary. In 1991, a massive urban conflagration blackened the Oakland and Berkeley hills, across the bay from San Francisco, killing 25 people and destroying 3,000 homes. In 1994, millions of acres of range and forestland in the Pacific Northwest and California went up in smoke following a long stretch of bone-dry weather and high temperatures. Fires charred thousands of acres in Colorado in 1996 and hundreds of acres in southern California in 1997, clearing vegetation and leaving both areas susceptible to deadly floods. Wildfires devastated southern California in 2003, creating one of the state's worst natural disasters, which smoldered across 750,000 acres, killed 20 people, and destroyed 3,000 homes. Conflagrations engulfed and destroyed parts of Texas and Oklahoma in 2005-06. And in October 2006, wild landfires tore wantonly across southeastern California, feasting on brittle plants and grasses and fanned by Santa Ana gusts. Residents were forced to abandon their homes to the flames. Unpredictably shifting "devil winds" killed firefighters battling the blaze.

The terror of a fast-racing wildfire is similar to that of a tornado, where speed and changes in direction trap victims before they have a chance to escape. As with all raging forces, they are not confined to one continent. Australia's dry climate and vegetation make it particularly vulnerable to bushfires. In 2003, a drought- and lightning-fueled wildfire swept into the nation's capital, Canberra, destroying hundreds of homes, forcing thousands to flee, and burning 50,000 acres. In the past 30 years, wildfires have killed hundreds in China, Indonesia, Mongolia, and Nepal, among other flash points. Raging forces are natural events on a monumental scale, but they can have deeply personal consequences. "I waken'd was with thund'ring noise / And piteous shrieks of dreadful voice. / That fearful sound of 'fire' and 'fire, ' / Let no man know is my Desire," wrote American Puritan poet Anne Bradstreet, who captured the particular horror of fire in "Verses Upon the Burning of Our House: July 10th, 1666," an event that, although historically remote, conveys across the ages the instant terror of nature's deadliest storms. Wildfires are more common today than in the past, as hotter temperatures dry the soil and warmer air produces more lightning.

sciences was a landmark in climatology. Aristotle's treatise contains a few observations that precede later scientific discoveries, such as his thoughts on geology: "If the sea is always advancing in one place and receding in another it is clear that the same parts of the whole earth are not always either sea or land, but that all this changes in course of time."

The factor of time plays a vital role in the distinction between weather and climate. One of the strongest expressions of the natural rhythm of seasons manifests in monsoons, highly variable winds, and rains that bookend the seasons, notably in southern Asia, but in Africa, the United States, Japan, China, South America, and other nations as well. Derived from the Arabic word mausim, meaning "season," a monsoon is a wind pattern that reverses direction with the seasons. In southern Asia, southwest winds bring heavy rains from May through September. The winds reverse in winter, breathing cool, dry air onto Asia and pouring torrents of rain on Indonesia, Australia, and other areas with northeast coastlines. The four-month summer monsoon yields 80 percent of India's total rainfall, sustaining far more than a billion people in neighboring nations. In most of rural Asia monsoon means the renewal of life; it is a mating call and a harbinger of fecundity. The monsoon is awaited with intensity, celebrated with joy, and bound in myth, proverb, and religion. In Indian poetry dark clouds bring happiness, while the winter sun delivers misery. "The clouds advance like rutting elephants," wrote the fifth-century Indian poet Kalidasa, "enormous and full of rain. / They come forward as kings among tumultuous armies; / their flags are lightning, the thunder is their drum."

Monsoons sustain life, but they can also be troublemakers. The North American Monsoon stretches from late May to September, originating over Mexico and spreading into the southwestern United States, setting off torrential mountain thunderstorms along the way. Heavy monsoon rains can help reduce wildfire threat, but they can also lead to excess winter plant growth, creating a new summer wildfire risk. Flash floods and deadly lightning storms increase in frequency and force during the monsoon season. The South American monsoon, meanwhile, brings tropical storms and flooding to Rio de Janeiro, Brazil. And monsoon-triggered landslides make a muddy and fatal mess of overgrazed and denuded mountainous regions.

When a monsoon fails to materialize, human catastrophe is just around the corner. Hindu astrologers call the tense and sun-scorched time before the monsoon *rohini*. It is a period of burning heat and dry winds that send grit and dust searing across the arid plains of the north, as dust storms lash villages and tempers flare in parched cities. A monsoon's failure mocks crops planted in anticipation of rain, turns fields to dust, and condemns communities to drought and famine.

"Everybody talks about the weather, but nobody does anything about it."
—Attributed to Mark Twain

When a monsoon bypassed parts of China in 1877, an estimated 10 million to 13 million people perished. Millions more died from monsoon-induced drought in India over the past three centuries. Economies, civilizations, and billions of lives ride on the promise of the monsoon—a promise as fickle and uncontrollable as any on Earth. The monsoon is not a hope to be relied upon, but a consummation devoutly to be wished.

CRAZY SEASONS

Suspended in time between weather, which changes daily, and climate, which changes gradually, is the periodic phenomenon of El Niño. Every two to seven years, typically around Christmastime—hence its nickname, the "The Boy Child" (referring to the baby Jesus), given by Peruvian fishermen—the trade winds over the western and central Pacific Ocean falter, and the surface layers of the ocean become warmer in the tropical eastern Pacific. During normal years the trade winds blow across the ocean from east to west, dragging warm surface water in the same direction. But during El Niño, weak winds allow ocean temperature patterns to reverse, bringing warm water to the eastern Pacific. As this heated equatorial water approaches the northern coastal regions of South America, it disrupts local weather patterns as well as marine biological processes, including the food chain. Heavy rains that typically pellet Australia and southern Asia become storms that pound usually dry eastern Pacific coastlines. El Niño's radical and aberrant weather patterns can produce a ripple effect that brings murderous drought to Australia, brush fires to Sumatra, heat waves to Mongolia, famine to North Korea, furious cyclones to South Pacific islands, disease outbreaks to Peru, floods to the southern United States and eastern Europe, and pestilence and food shortages to Africa.

The climatic calamity of an El Niño winter, brought on by the periodic warming of the eastern Pacific Ocean, is one part of a broad cycle of changes in the sea's surface temperature. Its cooler counterpart, La Niña (The Girl Child), frequently follows, bringing colder sea-surface temperatures and reversed climate patterns. Both events are part of a phenomenon called the El Niño-Southern Oscillation (ENSO), which combines ocean warming and atmospheric pressure changes that can deflect normal weather systems thousands of miles off course and last more than a year. A direct effect of ENSO is the catastrophic ocean warming that disrupts South American fisheries, leading to hardship and hunger. Less directly, El Niño cycles may influence and intensify storm systems and severe weather cycles, heightening the impact of natural events such as cyclones and drought.

El Niño and its associated torments are forces that have raged across the ages. Written records in Peru document the event's impact at least as far back as 1525, and researchers have found geologic evidence of the phenomenon in Peruvian coastal communities from at least 13,000 years ago. Epic droughts linked to the 1789-93 El Niño claimed at least 600,000 lives in just one region in India. Some historians argue that a series of El Niños in the late 19th century killed more people than the two World Wars of the 20th century combined. In 1878, a related drought brought famine to Asia, killing nine million in China and eight million in India. "The people's faces are black with hunger; they are dying by the thousands upon thousands. Women and girls and boys are openly offered for sale to any chance wayfarer," reported an Englishman in Shanghai.

More recent ENSO upturns have also produced deadly waves of destruction. The 1982-83 El Niño was a massive event that affected weather patterns on five continents, claimed the lives of about 2,000 people across the globe and cost $13 billion in destruction. A few million acres of Indonesia's rain forest burned, the monsoon season never arrived to cool southern India and Sri Lanka, cyclones ravaged French Polynesia, drought plagued Australia, floods triggered severe landslides and spread disease in Peru and Ecuador, and crops withered under the heat from cloudless skies that stretched from the Philippines to Botswana. The worst drought-related impacts on food production struck

Drenched bicycle commuters pedal through pelting rain in Patna, India, during the 2006 June-October monsoon season.

A luxury home in Laguna Niguel, California, is no match for a hillside eroded by heavy El Niño-generated rains in March 1998. El Niño is associated with a rise in sea-surface temperatures in the eastern Pacific that can wreak havoc on normal weather patterns: torrential rains in some areas, drought in another. El Niño can also have a devastating impact on marine life, which in turn affects fishermen dependent on large catches to make a living.

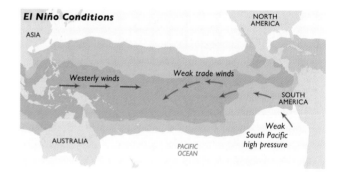

El Niño Conditions

NORTH AMERICA

ASIA

Westerly winds

Weak trade winds

SOUTH AMERICA

Weak South Pacific high pressure

AUSTRALIA

PACIFIC OCEAN

Sea surface temperature below 77°F (25°C)

Sea surface temperature between 77°F and 82.4°F

Sea surface temperature above 82.4°F (28°C)

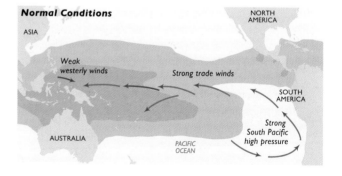

Normal Conditions

NORTH AMERICA

ASIA

Weak westerly winds

Strong trade winds

SOUTH AMERICA

Strong South Pacific high pressure

AUSTRALIA

PACIFIC OCEAN

Ethiopia, leading to the famine that gripped the land and crippled more than seven million people.

Scientists were better prepared, having honed their predictive abilities, for the next titanic El Niño, which arrived quickly and with violent force in 1997-98. This was the strongest El Niño on record, and it developed more rapidly than any in the past. "It rose out of the tropical Pacific in late 1997, bearing more energy than a million Hiroshima bombs. By the time it had run its course eight months later, the giant El Niño of 1997-98 had deranged weather patterns around the world, killed an estimated 2,100 people, and caused at least 33 billion dollars in property damage," wrote Curt Suplee in *National Geographic*. Mudslides and flash floods devastated communities from California to Mississippi, storms pounded the Gulf Coast, and tornadoes ripped across Florida. Indonesia suffered drought, and forest fires carbonized Sumatra, Borneo, Malaysia, and vast stretches of the Amazon. Malaria flared up in Peru. Central Europe flooded, and Kenya received record rainfall.

Whether global warming will exacerbate the effects of El Niño is a hot topic of debate. Scientists are in agreement that El Niños have become more frequent and progressively warmer over the past century. And it is likely that future ENSO events will pack a punch as deadly as—if not deadlier than—past El Niños. Human activities often increase, rather than protect against, the impacts of these climatic calamities. Shifting settlement, increasing population trends, and radically increased logging leading to deforestation in the Philippines exponentially increased the effects of La Niña rainfall in 2003-04, leading to landslides that claimed the lives of 2,000 people. Future events have the potential to make this devastation seem like a small yawn from the stormy siblings.

SCORCHED EARTH

In September 2006, monster swarms of locusts plagued Cancún, the Mexican resort town, forming airborne insect armies that devoured everything in sight and gravely threatened a coastal Caribbean region still recovering from devastating Hurricane Wilma, which struck the year before. Locusts are grasshoppers that have entered a swarming phase, and can quickly strip fields bare over large distances. Armed with motorized backpack pumps that shot chemicals into the teeming, ravenous enemy masses, villagers eventually won their war against a plague that affected nearly 2,500 acres of farmland in the Yucatán Peninsula. But the locust sorties, which typically invade the region in four-year cycles, will return to attack another day.

"They are nature's blitzkrieg army: Absolutely fearless, never considering retreat, equally at ease in the air or on the ground, they wage their lightning wars

> Back in my hometown
> They would have cleared the floor
> Just to watch the rain come down
> They're such sky-oriented people
> Geared to changing weather
>
> —JONI MITCHELL, "PAPRIKA PLAINS"

Clouds of uncountable locusts formed a plague of biblical proportion that swarmed across Dubbo, New South Wales, Australia, in 2004.

by banding together in the millions, suddenly attacking and overrunning one area, then swiftly moving on to another," writes National Geographic's Tom Melham. "They are one of man's oldest and costliest enemies; mere mention of their name still conjures chilling visions of dense, living blizzards blotting out the sun, of multitudes falling to earth and streaming from horizon to horizon, leaving a wake of ravaged crops, leafless and barked trees, and famine." Locust invasions are one of the ten biblical plagues of Egypt, devastating calamities inflicted by God more than 3,000 years ago to persuade Egypt's Pharaoh to permit the Israelite slaves to leave, as recorded in the Book of Exodus.

An insect plague is a complex outbreak where the population of a species suddenly erupts, causes instant vexation and destruction, and then just as quickly disappears. The desert locust, one of 7,000 species of grasshopper, has persistently plagued every civilization of Egypt, the Fertile Crescent, and the Indus Valley. Records of their voracious visitations have been left in eighth-century B.C. bas-relief by Assyrian artists at Nineveh and tomb carvers at Saqqara in Lower Egypt. Arab farmers frequently refer to locust swarms as the Army of

Allah, and the chaos these famished fliers deliver to their current range—from northwestern Africa, to India and
Bangladesh—has only increased as agricultural techniques
have consolidated farmlands. A widespread locust plague
in 1958 destroyed an estimated 167,000 tons of grain in
Ethiopia alone, contributing to a critical food shortage.

> "For they covered the face of the whole earth, so that the land was darkened; and they did eat every herb of the land, and all the fruits of the trees."
>
> —EXODUS 10:15

Desert locusts do not make their way to North America, but plagues of
pinebark beetles, spruce budworms, fire ants, and grasshoppers periodically ravage the United States. In 1518, a plague of fire ants caused an environmental
crisis on Hispaniola (present-day Dominican Republic). The Mormon cricket,
a long-horned, flightless grasshopper, was the bane of Utah's first settlers, who
watched in horror as menacing mobs began devouring their crop of ripening winter wheat in 1848. The crickets were stopped only by a precipitous flock of hundreds of sea gulls that feasted on the crickets before the pests had destroyed all
of the wheat. These masticating marauders have returned periodically to destroy
and disappear. Cricket plagues hit Utah eight years in a row from the late 1930s
to the early 1940s, and continue to threaten the region today.

Many other plague creatures have come as a result not just of natural tenac-
ity, but of human interference. In 1869, a Harvard astronomer with an interest
in silk brought a European moth species to Massachusetts, When these moths
escaped and multiplied, they initiated recurrent plagues of North America's
worst caterpillar pest, the gypsy moth, which can defoliate forests almost
overnight. Other alien insects that have plagued North America include the
aggressive and venomous South American fire ant, the notorious Japanese beetle, and the fungus-carrying European elm bark beetle, vector for Dutch elm disease. Around the world, the colonization of alien animals has frequently come
to disastrous ends. Australia's and New Zealand's bane has been the European
rabbit, brought by Engishmen to remind them of home. By the 1880s, the rabbit population was out of control. Even the introduction of a bunny virus, myx-
omatosis, failed to eradicate the highly reproductive rabbits, and so the plague
marches on, wounded and somewhat contained, but not defeated.

BLACK DEATH

As Italian Renaissance chronicler Giovanni Boccaccio observed, Europe's 14th-
century plague years were a time of ghastly visions and horrific demise.
"Consecrated churchyards did not suffice for the burial of the vast multitude
of bodies, which were heaped by the hundreds in vast trenches, like goods in a
ships hold and covered with a little earth." Pandemics—of which there have
been three in the past 1,500 years—are epidemics that reach biologically devastating proportions. One of history's greatest scourges was the "Black Death"

Worst Epidemics in History

Illness	Year	Death Toll
Black Death	1347-80s	75 million
AIDS	1981-	27.8 million *
Influenza	1918-20	21.6 million
Bubonic plague	1896-1948	12 million
Typhus	1914-15	3 million
Plague of Justinian	541-590	millions **
Cholera	1826-37	millions **
	1846-60	
	1893-94	
Smallpox	1530-45	1 million +

* Up to 2005
** No precise figures available

Source: Russell Ash, *The Top 10 of Everything: 2006*, DK Publishing

Ten Killer Diseases in the Developing World

Annual Death Toll	Illness
4 million+	Lower respiratory infections
3 million+	HIV/AIDS
1-5 million	Malaria
2.2 million	Diarrhea
2 million	Tuberculosis
530,000	Measles
200,000-300,000	Whooping cough
214,000	Tetanus
174,000	Meningitis
157,000	Syphilis

Source: World Health Organization

and "Destroying Angel" of bubonic plague, named for its painful, bruiselike buboes, or lymph gland swellings. From its emergence in Central Asia, the bacterium *Yersinia pestis* traveled by infected rats and fleas around the globe, ravaging human populations. "They died by the hundreds both day and night," wrote Agnolo di Tura, of Siena, who buried his five children during the same plague observed by Boccaccio. "[T]here were also those who were so sparsely covered with earth that the dogs dragged them forth and devoured many bodies throughout the city. There was no one who wept for any death, for all awaited death. And so many died that all believed it was the end of the world."

Pandemics are not the end of the world, though they can quickly cause the utter collapse of societies. The first recorded smallpox epidemic occurred in 1350 B.C., during the Egyptian-Hittite War. Greek historian Herodotus credits a pestilence that may have been the bubonic plague with killing some 300,000 invading Persians in 480 B.C. Greek historian Thucydides survived a bout with a disease (most likely typhus) that afflicted the people of Athens in 430 B.C., during the Peloponnesian War against their great rival Sparta. This illness, which killed almost a third of the Athenian population—including the city's leader, Pericles—over four years, became the world's first recorded pandemic. The Roman Empire crumbled not just to barbarian attackers, but also to bubonic plague, most likely conveyed by the same magnificent highway systems that led to the empire's former glory. A bubonic pandemic, the "Plague of Justinian," emerged from Egypt in the sixth century to engulf the Byzantine Empire and most of the known Western world; perhaps 40 percent of Constantinople's entire population died. Plagues rebuffed the Fourth Crusade before it reached Jerusalem, and a pandemic festered in the 1300s and raged for 300 years, invading China, India, and Europe. In just five years, the Black Death of 1347 to 1352 killed 25 million people, perhaps one of every four Europeans. One of its last surges claimed 70,000 lives in 17th-century London. High death rates were exacerbated by poor hygiene and an inability to understand the spread of the disease by rats and fleas.

Bubonic plague has exploded periodically throughout history, but it is not alone as an epidemic killer. Malaria, typhoid, typhus, tuberculosis, cholera, yellow fever, dengue fever, measles, meningitis, smallpox, forms of influenza, and HIV/AIDS have inflicted civilizations across the ages. Epidemics (from the Greek for "upon people") are outbreaks of contractible disease that spread quickly through a human population. Pandemics are outbreaks with global reach. Bubonic plague is blamed for the death of perhaps 250 million people, but other infectious diseases have had similarly tortuous and torturous histories. Fifteenth-century European explorers to Central and South America brought more than just imperial visions; they also carried smallpox, measles, and typhus, which decimate local populations. Between 1518 and 1568, pandemic diseases are said to have caused the population of Mexico to fall from 20 million to 3 million. The worldwide death toll of smallpox, which raged into the 20th century, is estimated at more than 300 million people.

In the 20th century, three flu pandemics killed tens of millions. The first and worst, the Spanish flu, started in 1918 and moved across the globe with breathtaking speed, killing more than 50 million people—more than had died in World War I, which was coming to an end when the disease disappeared. Other deadly influenza outbreaks followed, including the 1957 and 1968 Asian pandemics, which together killed an estimated three million people. Today influenza kills about 250,000 to 500,000 worldwide each year—36,000 of them in the United States. Malaria, which affects more than 300 million annually, kills an estimated

An apocalyptic image from the 15th-century Nuremberg Chronicle depicts the horrors that await humanity at the end of time.

London's Great Smog of 1952 made walking a perilous endeavor and driving nearly suicidal.

2 million people each year. Worldwide, more than two billion people are infected with tuberculosis, and two million die of it each year. Some 40 million people in the world live with HIV/AIDS, which kills more than 3 million annually. Ebola hemorrhagic fever, severe acute respiratory syndrome (SARS), and West Nile virus are potential future epidemic threats.

Many tropical viruses and their host insects, monkeys, waterfowl, or other animals have lived and reproduced for millennia with limited global impact. But when a microbe jumps from a longtime animal host to a human, it may cease being a harmless parasite and infect a human as a pathogen, setting off a deadly chain of events. Urbanization, changes in agriculture, encroachment on wilderness areas, and high-speed transport are among the human activities that can swiftly promote virulent pathogen transmission. Such is the case for the deadly H5N1 avian flu virus, which has the potential to jump from bird to person, sparking a pandemic that could quickly sweep the globe, wipe out human populations, and devastate economies. Estimated deaths in such a pandemic range from 7.4 million to an apocalyptic 150 million, extrapolating 1918 Spanish flu deaths to today's population.

BURNING DOWN THE HOUSE

Londoners, long accustomed to the menace and mirth of ground-hugging clouds—whimsically known as pea soupers by many—initially took the descent of a thick black mist on December 5, 1952, in stride. But this cold fog was no mere mass of minute water droplets. Locals soon realized that their city was enveloped in a shallow, caustic cocoon that kept sulfur dioxide and other pollutants trapped in a deadly inversion layer immobilized under a warmer layer of air. For five suffocating days the smog thickened as concentrations of pollutants, coal smoke in particular, built up dramatically. The smog was so thick that it blotted out the sun, driving became treacherous, trains stopped running, cattle in nearby Smithfield were asphyxiated, and film screenings were canceled because of the impenetrable, clinging air. At least 4,000 people—and as many as 12,000—died of asthma, bronchitis, and pneumonia exacerbated by what was variously known as the Great Smog or the Big Smoke.

The galling disaster of the smog, fueled by human consumption and tragically empowered by atmospheric misfortune, left a positive legacy by forming an important impetus to the modern environmental movement. The catastrophe spurred legislation that mandated reduced emissions and cleaner fuels and is remembered today as an early alarm to the lethal potential of air pollution.

"How many valiant men, how many fair ladies, breakfast with their kinfolk and the same night supped with their ancestors in the next world! They sickened by the thousands daily, and died unattended and without help. Many died in the open street, others dying in their houses, made it known by the stench of their rotting bodies."

—Giovanni Boccaccio

"Things that normally happen in geologic time are happening during the span of a human lifetime. It's like watching the Statue of Liberty melt," Daniel Fagre, a climate scientist with the U.S. Geological Survey, tells *National Geographic* magazine. Fagre studied Glacier National Park in Montana, which was home to an estimated 150 glaciers at its founding in 1910. Today the park has fewer than 30 glaciers, and most of those remaining have shrunk by two-thirds. Within the next 30 years, most, if not all, will most likely disappear. Similar tales of meltdown abound around the world. Two of Africa's highest peaks—Mount Kilimanjaro and Mount Kenya—may lose their ice cover within the next 50 years if deforestation and industrial pollution are not stopped. Glaciers in the Himalaya, Europe, Alaska, and South America are rapidly receding. Arctic and Antarctic ice shelves have steadily fractured in recent decades, threatening to contribute to rising sea levels.

And the effects of global warming are not limited to ice-cover meltdown. One-third of China is now suffering from acid rain caused by rapid industrial growth and pollution. As the oceans get warmer, storms will most likely get stronger. Atlantic and Pacific cyclones since the 1970s have increased in duration and intensity by about 50 percent. Forty years ago, Africa's Lake Chad was the sixth largest lake in the world, as large as Lake Erie. But now it is only about one-twentieth of that size, as a result of lowered rainfall and human factors. Meanwhile, the disappearance of Lake Chad's water was accompanied by dry cycles that helped ignite the simmering hostility in nearby Darfur. Global warming strains the boundary between humans and microbes, creating vulnerability to new and unfamiliar diseases and new strains of diseases once under control. Increasing temperature could lead to the extinction of some species, which would find it increasingly difficult to find viable habitats. Global warming causes temperatures and sea levels to rise, permafrost to thaw, rivers to run dry, winds to shift, wildfires to blaze, summers to extend, coral reefs to bleach, exotic species to invade, and coastlines to erode.

". . . [t]here is strong scientific consensus that human activities are changing the Earth's climate. Scientists overwhelmingly agree that the Earth is getting warmer, that this trend is caused by people, and that if we continue to pump greenhouse gases into the atmosphere, the warming will be increasingly harmful," writes Al Gore in *An Inconvenient Truth*. "Many people today still assume—mistakenly—that the Earth is so big that we human beings cannot possibly have any major impact on the way our planet's ecological system operates. That assertion may have been true at one time, but it's

"Global warming, along with the cutting and burning of forests and other critical habitats, is causing a loss of living species at a level comparable to the extinction event that wiped out the dinosaurs 65 million years ago. That event was believed to have been caused by a giant asteroid. This time it is not an asteroid colliding with the Earth and wreaking havoc; it is us."

—AL GORE, *AN INCONVENIENT TRUTH*

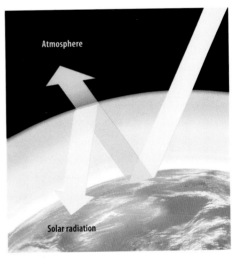

Industrial smokestacks disgorge black chemical clouds of polluted haze that will linger for extended periods in Earth's atmosphere, soaking up and trapping solar radiation in the planet-warming process known as the greenhouse effect. Carbon dioxide, which is emitted by the burning of fossil fuels, is a significant and threatening greenhouse gas.

Atmosphere

Solar radiation

not the case anymore. We have grown so numerous and our technologies have become so powerful that we are now capable of having a significant influence on many parts of the Earth's environment." And the explosion in human population—which increases by more than 75 million people a year—has only begun. From 2006 to 2050, the world's population is projected to grow from 6.5 billion people to 9.1 billion, a 40 percent increase. Since per-person energy use is likely to increase, total greenhouse gas emissions (mainly carbon dioxide) could well double by 2050. This rapid population rise drives demand for food, water, and energy—and for all our natural resources, placing enormous pressure on vulnerable areas such as tropical rain forests.

Global warming refers to the rise in the average temperature of the entire Earth's surface, including the temperatures of our oceans, due to increased levels of greenhouse gases. The world has always undergone periodic fluctuations in temperature, but the rapid accumulation of greenhouse gases in the atmosphere due to human activities is responsible for a more rapid increase in temperature over our planet. Of all the gases that make up Earth's atmosphere, greenhouse gases are a vital group because they permit energy in the form of visible light to pass, while absorbing invisible heat waves, or infrared light from the sun. The sunlight's energy gets converted to heat in the ground, which in turn radiates back toward space as infrared waves. When this infrared energy becomes trapped in Earth's atmosphere, it further warms the air, ground, and oceans. This natural greenhouse effect originally warmed Earth enough to develop and sustain life. But from the industrial age onward, the enormous burning of fossil fuels (coal, oil, and gas) blankets the atmosphere with higher levels of carbon dioxide and other gases that retain a larger percentage of surface heat. The basic result is that the average temperature of Earth's atmosphere has crept up in tandem with the increased concentration of greenhouse gases. Globally the temperature is up more than 1°F in the past century, but some of the coldest, most remote spots have warmed much more. And since climate directly affects agriculture, water supplies, and human health, this change threatens to disrupt civilization and security for centuries to come.

The impacts of climate change will not be the same everywhere. Some areas of the globe—such as northern Europe—might actually become colder. As ice melts and warmer seawater expands, oceans will rise, endangering worldwide more than a hundred million people who live within three feet of mean sea level. Many low-lying South Sea islands risk flooding with only four inches of increased sea level. Three-quarters of coastal Louisiana's wetlands would be destroyed at 1.5 feet. In Bangladesh, at just over three feet of rise, 70 million people would be displaced. The rise in sea levels brings a concomitant intensification of storms and expansion of drought zones, leading to devastating human consequences such as food shortages, shrinking water supplies, and refugee crises. These in turn may trigger wars over dwindling resources. Global warming can bring a shift in seasons—shorter winters, longer summers—that greatly affects the habitat and natural processes of flora and fauna worldwide, as well as the precarious ecological balance between flora and fauna.

Mark Lynas, author of *High Tide: The Truth About Our Climate Crisis,* says that we need to end our reliance on fossil fuel consumption if we are to survive. "I think there is a 50-50 chance we can avoid a devastating rise in global temperature," Lynas says. "If you were diagnosed with a potentially deadly disease and given those odds, you wouldn't hesitate to go through treatment. So why wouldn't we respond the same way when the whole of the planet is at stake?" Lynas has been working on a book called *Six Degrees,* which outlines what to expect from a warming world, degree by degree. A rise of only 10°F would cause the destruction of most coral reefs and many mountain glaciers, Lynas says. A 30°F rise would result in the collapse of the Amazon rain forest, the disappearance of Greenland's ice sheet, and the creation of deserts across the midwestern United States and southern Africa. Most life on Earth—including much human life—would disappear with warming of 60°F.

Lynas bases many of his projections on the Earth's geological past. "The only other time our planet warmed by 60°," Lynas says, almost 100 percent of the world's species were "wiped out." He adds, "That was 251 million years ago, and it took another 50 million years for biodiversity to return to its previous level. In fact, since life on Earth began, every episode of mass extinction has been associated with a change in climate. This time, the greenhouse gases created by humans are causing warming to occur exponentially faster. And since half the world's forests have been cut down, and most of the natural land surface

The resettlement of hardy plants, such as this graminea growing near ice cliffs at high elevation in Bolivia, correlates with global warming and the retreat of glaciers.

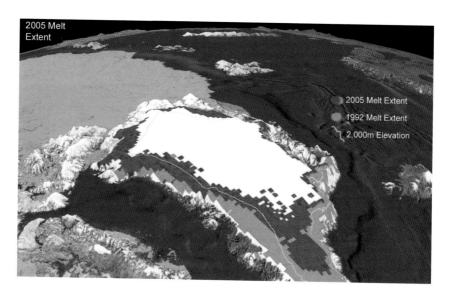

The total melt area of the Greenland ice sheet reached a record extent in 2005, in yet another indication of increasing global temperatures due to accelerated climate change.

Global Warming, by the Numbers

1 degree: average global increase in temperature (Fahrenheit) in the past century

150 (estimated): number of glaciers in Glacier National Park in 1910

fewer than 30: current number of glaciers in Glacier National Park

2007: predicted year when last glacier will disappear

80 percent: amount of melting of the famous snows of Kilimanjaro

10 percent: total decrease in the extent of Arctic sea ice over the past 30 years

$^1/_{10}$ inch: amount global sea level rises each year

25 square miles: amount of wetlands Louisiana loses every year to energy

1998, 2002, 2003, 2001, 1997: hottest years on record, starting with the hottest

20 feet: amount sea level would rise if the west Antarctic ice sheet broke up

4 to 35 inches: amount sea level will rise by the end of this century

3 feet: amount of sea level rise that would displace 70 million residents of Bangladesh

1.5 feet: amount of sea level rise that would destroy 75 percent of Louisiana's wetlands

23 cubic miles: annual water runoff from Alaska glaciers (biggest contributor to global sea level rise)

100 million: number of people across the globe who live within three feet of mean sea level

8.8°F: winter average temperature increase on west Antarctic Peninsula since 1950 (4.5°F annual)

4: number of polar or mountain species at risk due to global warming (polar bear, gelada baboon, pygmy possum, monarch butterfly)

Source: *National Geographic* magazine (September 2004)

destroyed, the regulatory systems which keep climate habitable can't function. It's as though we've turned up the thermostat after disabling the safety mechanisms. In this precarious position, a mass extinction now would be worse than any in the past."

> "Observe always that everything is the result of change, and get used to thinking that there is nothing Nature loves so well as to change existing forms and to make new ones like them."
>
> —MARCUS AURELIUS, *MEDITATIONS*

How should we respond to this crisis? On a positive note, controls on deleterious compounds, such as chlorofluorocarbons, have helped the ozone hole over Antarctica—which reached its biggest and deepest size ever in 2006, permitting the sun's harmful ultraviolet rays to enter the Earth's atmosphere—begin a trend toward shrinkage. Concentrations of ozone-depleting chemicals in the lower atmosphere have been declining since 1995, and scientists estimate the ozone hole will be completely recovered by about 2068. Such broad-ranging initiatives must be undertaken to combat a scourge that threatens to destroy the planet. "The message is clear. Global climate change must take its place alongside those threats—conflict, poverty, the proliferation of deadly weapons—that have traditionally monopolized first-order political attention," said U.N. Secretary General Kofi Annan in 2006. While governing bodies focus on multinational efforts to curb global warming—efforts such as the Kyoto Protocol, an international treaty that targets the reduction of greenhouse gas emissions, and markets for carbon offsets—individuals can play an Earth-saving role by driving fuel-efficient cars, replacing incandescent lightbulbs with fluorescent ones, turning down the thermostat on water heaters, reducing water consumption, and recycling. In many ways, going green has never been easier—but consuming less on a per capita basis remains a matter of judicious, mindful, and sustained self-control.

THE END OF THE WORLD

Today the word "apocalypse" refers generally to the end of the world. But in Jewish and Christian literature, this word—whose Greek root means "the lifting of the veil"—means a revelation of hidden wisdom concerning the destiny of humankind that precedes the end of an age. It's an important distinction: the end of an age versus the end of all time. Some religious interpretations of end-time refer to Armageddon, the apocalyptic battle between good and evil mentioned in the Book of Revelation. Islamic belief refers to Qiyamah, the Last Judgment, which precedes humanity's unraveling. Other stories, such as the Old Testament tale of Noah and the ark miraculously surviving a flood sent by God as punishment for the world's sinfulness, refer as much to the end of an age as they do to the beginning of a new one. In Norse mythology, Ragnarök ("fate of the gods") is the epic battle at the end of the world. So much doom, so little time, it seems. Yet for pragmatists the existential peril implied in human-extinction scenarios makes choosing the correct word for the end of the world seem almost a trivial pursuit next to just staying alive.

Shock waves of devastation have carried civilization like flotsam across the ages, and we're still here. From the dawn of civilization, catastrophes have endangered humans on personal, regional, and global scales. Instant death during the plague years, for example, looked apocalyptic, but somehow civilization survived. Massive volcanic eruptions may have doomed Atlantis, but the world at large moved on. In the frozen mountainside on the island of Svalbard, Norway is building an Arctic "doomsday vault," designed to house all known varieties of the world's crops, safeguarding diversity in the event of a global catastrophe. More than 100 countries have backed the vault, which will store seeds, packaged in foil, at subzero temperatures. Yet, so far, this investment of time and care is just a precaution.

Space scientists indicate that certain events in space—galactic impact, solar flares, black hole explosions, asteroid collisions—will cause life on Earth to end, but since these catastrophes are not scheduled for many billions of years in the future, it will be hard to hold the prognosticators to their word. Earth scientists warn of intense global warming, ice ages, mega-tsunamis, super volcanoes, and nuclear holocausts. Biologists fear global pandemics, antibiotic resistance, human infertility, overpopulation, and long-term famine. Science fictionists fear "gray goo," a hypothetical scenario in which out-of-control self-replicating robots consume all living matter on Earth while building more of themselves. In *Cat's Cradle,* writer Kurt Vonnegut conceived of ice-nine, a fictional crystal seed that freezes water at ambient temperatures, destroying the world as we know it.

Life is the handmaiden to death, and every birth on Earth is sure to meet its end. Old alarms, such as the rumblings of Vesuvius, engage in an endless danse macabre with present catastrophes, like global warming, which may already have caused extinctions in populations of frogs, butterflies, ocean corals, and polar birds. At times, the end of life on Earth seems both inevitable and near, even if that end comes, as T. S. Eliot wrote, "not with a bang but a whimper." And yet scientist James J. Lovelock, who has long criticized our catastrophic reliance on fossil fuels, sounds a hopeful message about humans' ability to survive climate change—even when that change renders most of the world inhospitable. "The human species has been on the planet for a million years now. We've gone through seven major climatic changes that are equivalent to this. The ice ages were shifts in climate comparable with this one that's coming. And we've survived. That series of glaciations and interglacials put the pressures on us to select the kind of human that could adapt. And we're the progeny of them. And we're just up against a new and different stress. Maybe we'll come out better." For our own sake, let's hope so. ∎

An Indonesian man navigates downtown
Jakarta through an anti-mosquito fog in
2005. A global explosion of viral infection,
such as dengue fever, is an increasing threat
to populations around the world.

Billowing clouds gather over Port Moresby, Papua New Guinea, promising much needed rain for a city that becomes a dust bowl in the dry season.

Index

Acknowledgments

Raging Forces is dedicated to Matt Voorhees, Chris Dorobek, and Daisy the Amazing Beagle: my boundlessly supportive, endlessly affectionate extended family.

With special gratitude to Chris Farmer, who weathered the storm. Thanks to amazing Barbara Brownell Grogan. Deep appreciation to my scientific colleagues and writerly friends who have each made remarkable contributions of their own: P. F. Kluge and Pamela Hollie; John Midgley; Elizabeth Midgley and Sidney Weintraub; Perry Lentz; Deborah Laycock; Jack Finefrock; Shannon Wilkinson; Giles, Meredith, and Nebuliana Roblyer; Grant Wiggins and Olivia Sainz; Jill Muffy Pollack; Geoffrey Saunders Schramm, Ph.D.; Johnna Rizzo; tornado chaser McKenzie Funk; Grace Funk; Benson Wilder; Ris Lacoste; Brian Groh; Suzanne King; Brett House; volcanologist Gregg Helvey; Lora Price; Kyeh Kim; Jessica Buckholz; Ann Loeffler; Jed Sundwall; Teena Purohit; Valerie Hletko; Katie Wood; Blake Gwinn; geologist Johan Bergenas; Ellen Farmer; explorer Julian Smith; Laura Fravel; Pat McGeehan; and Malcolm Auchincloss. With cheer to the Steinberg-Bernstein family,and Lorraine, Spencer, Prudy, Bub, Christy, Paige, Sophia, and Sarah Stone.

Credits

Further Reading

Books

Amery, Colin, and Brian Curran. *The Lost World of Pompeii.* Getty Trust Publications, 2002.

Ballard, Robert D. *Exploring Our Living Planet.* National Geographic Society, 1983.

Brinkley, Douglas. *The Great Deluge: Hurricane Katrina, New Orleans, and the Mississippi Gulf Coast.* William Morrow, 2006.

Burt, Christopher C. *Extreme Weather: A Guide and Record Book.* W. W. Norton, 2004.

Carson, Rachel. *Silent Spring,* 40th anniversary ed. Mariner Books, 2002.

Cerveny, Randy. *Freaks of the Storm: The World's Strangest True Weather Stories, From Flying Cows to Stealing Thunder.* Thunder's Mouth Press, 2006.

Clair, Jean, ed. *Cosmos: From Romanticism to the Avant-Garde.* Prestel, 1999.

Clark, Ella E. *Indian Legends of the Pacific Northwest.* University of California Press, 2003.

Darwin, Charles. *Voyage of the Beagle,* Ed. Janet Browne. Penguin Classics, 1989.

Decker, Robert, and Barbara Decker. *Volcanoes in America's National Parks.* Odyssey Guides, 2001.

Earthquake. Planet Earth. Time-Life Books, 1982.

Egan, Timothy. *The Worst Hard Time: The Untold Story of Those Who Survived the Great American Dust Bowl.* Houghton Mifflin, 2006.

Emanuel, Kerry. *Divine Wind: The History and Science of Hurricanes.* Oxford University Press, 2005.

Fagan, Brian M. *The Long Summer: How Climate Changed Civilization.* Basic Books, 2004.

Flannery, Tim. *The Weather Makers: How Man Is Changing the Climate and What It Means for Life on Earth.* Atlantic Monthly Press, 2006.

Forces of Change: A New View of Nature. Smithsonian Institution and National Geographic Society, 2000.

Gore, Al. *An Inconvenient Truth: The Planetary Emergency of Global Warming and What We Can Do About It.* Rodale Press, 2006.

Kolbert, Elizabeth. *Field Notes From a Catastrophe: Man, Nature, and Climate Change.* Bloomsbury, 2006.

Kovach, Robert, and Bill McGuire. *Firefly Guide to Global Hazards: A Complete Reference Guide to the Natural Hazards That Endanger Life on Earth.* Firefly Books, 2004.

Langone, John, Bruce Stutz, and Andrea Gianopoulos. *Theories for Everything: An Illustrated History of Science From the Invention of Numbers to the Cosmic Triangle.* National Geographic Society, 2006.

Lee, Laura. *Blame It On the Rain: How the Weather Has Changed History.* Harper Paperbacks, 2006.

Linden, Eugene. *The Winds of Change: Climate, Weather, and the Destruction of Civilizations.* Simon and Schuster, 2006.

Lovelock, James. *The Revenge of Gaia: Earth's Climate Crisis and the Fate of Humanity.* Basic Books, 2006.

Lynas, Mark. *High Tide: The Truth About Our Climate Crisis.* Picador, 2004.

Mort, Terry, ed. *Mark Twain on Travel.* Lyons Press, 2005.

National Geographic Almanac of Geography. National Geographic Society, 2005.

Nature on the Rampage: Our Violent Earth. National Geographic Society, 1986.

Nature's Extremes: Inside the Great Natural Disasters That Shape Life on Earth. Time, 2006.

Oman, Anne. *Weather: Nature in Motion.* National Geographic Society, 2005.

Powers of Nature. National Geographic Society, 1978.

Raging Forces: Earth in Upheaval. National Geographic Society, 1995.

Restless Earth: Nature's Awesome Powers. National Geographic Society, 1997.

Robinson, Andrew. *Earth Shock: Hurricanes, Volcanoes, Earthquakes, Tornadoes and Other Forces of Nature.* Thames and Hudson, 2002.

Rosenfeld, Jeffrey P. *Eye of the Storm: Inside the World's Deadliest Hurricanes, Tornadoes, and Blizzards.* Basic Books, 2003.

Sigurdsson, Haraldur. *Melting the Earth: The History of Ideas on Volcanic Eruptions.* Oxford University Press, 1999.

Standish, David. *Hollow Earth.* Da Capo Press, 2006.

Stone, George W. *Extreme Earth.* Collins, 2003.

Storm. Planet Earth. Time-Life Books, 1982.

Suplee, Curt. *Milestones of Science: The History of Humankind's Greatest Ideas.* National Geographic Society, 2000.

Thoreau, Henry David. *Walden* and "Resistance to Civil Government," Norton Critical Edition, 2nd ed. W. W. Norton, 1992.

Volcano. Planet Earth. Time-Life Books, 1982.

Volcanoes: A Firefly Guide. Firefly Books, 2003.

Vonnegut, Kurt. *Cat's Cradle.* Dell Publishing, 1963.

———. *Galápagos: A Novel.* Delacorte Press, 1985.

Young, Louise B. *Islands: Portraits of Miniature Worlds.* W. H. Freeman, 1999.

Wallechinsky, David. *The People's Almanac Presents the 20th Century,* rev. update ed. Overlook Press, 1999.

Willis, Roy. *World Mythology.* Henry Holt, 1996.

Wilson, E. O. *The Creation: An Appeal to Save Life on Earth.* W. W. Norton, 2006.

Winchester, Simon. *A Crack in the Edge of the World: America and the Great California Earthquake of 1906.* Harper Perennial, 2006.

———. *Krakatoa: The Day the World Exploded,* August 27, 1883. HarperCollins, 2003.

Zeilinga de Boer, Jelle, and Donald Theodore Sanders. *Volcanoes in Human History: The Far-Reaching Effects of Seismic Disruptions.* Princeton University Press, 2004.

Magazines and Newspapers

Achenbach, Joel. "The Next Big One," *National Geographic.* (April 2006), 120-147.

Appenzeller, Tim. "Tracking the Next Killer Flu." *National Geographic.* (October 2005), 2-31.

Blakeslee, Sandra. "Ancient Crash, Epic Wave." *New York Times,* November 14, 2006.

Bourne, Joel K., Jr. "Ol Doinyo Langai." *National Geographic.* (January 2003), 34-49.

Brookes, Tim. "Fire and Rain: Forecasting the Chaos of Weather," *National Geographic.* (June 2005), 90-109.

Findley, Rowe. "Mount St. Helens: Nature on Fast Forward." *National Geographic.* (May 2000), 106-125.

Glanz, James. "Eruption Science: Volcanoes as Labs." *New York Times,* November 18, 2003.

"Global Warning: Signs from Earth." *National Geographic.* (September 2004), 2-75.

Gore, Rick. "Cascadia: Living on Fire." *National Geographic.* (May 1998), 6-37.

———. "Wrath of the Gods: A History Forged by Disaster." *National Geographic.* (July 2000), 52-71.

Graves, William. "Earthquake!" *National Geographic.* (July 1964), 112-39.

Grove, Noel. "A Village Fights for its Life." *National Geographic.* (July 1973), 40-67.

———. "Volcanoes: Crucibles of Creation." *National Geographic.* (December 1992), 2-41.

Holland, Jennifer S. "Red Hot Hawaii: Volcanoes National Park." *National Geographic.* (October 2004), 2-24.

"Hope in Hell: Deadly Delay." *National Geographic.* (December 2005), 2-45.

James, Jamie. "The Second Act of Krakatoa." *National Geographic Adventure.* (October 2003), 74-82, 99-100.

Miller, Peter. "Tornado!" *National Geographic.* (June 1987), 690-715.

Mydans, Carl. "Disaster in Japan." *Life.* (July 12, 1948), 19-23.

Newcott, William R. "Lightning: Nature's High-Voltage Spectacle." *National Geographic.* (July 1993), 83-103.

Oldenburg, Don. "A Sense of Doom: Animal Instinct for Disaster." *Washington Post,* January 8, 2005.

Parfit, Michael. "Living With Natural Hazards." *National Geographic.* (July 1998), 2-39.

Pinna, Marco. "Etna Ignites." *National Geographic.* (February 2002), 68-87.

Reid, T. R. "Kobe Wakes to a Nightmare." *National Geographic.* (July 1995), 112-36.

Revkin, Andrew C. "A Conversation with James Lovelock," *New York Times,* September 12, 2006.

"St. Helens: Mountain with a Death Wish." *National Geographic.* (January 1981), 3-33.

Stager, Curt. "Africa's Great Rift." *National Geographic.* (May 1990), 2-41.

Suplee, Curt. "El Niño/La Niña: Nature's Vicious Cycle." *National Geographic.* (March 1999), 72-87, 93-95.

Vesilind, Priit J. "Chasing Tornadoes." *National Geographic.* (April 2004), 2-37.

———. "Monsoons." *National Geographic.* (December 1984). 712-47.

———. "Once and Future Fury: California's Volcanic North." *National Geographic.* (October 2001), 68-83.

Webster, Donovan. "Inside the Volcano." *National Geographic.* (November 2000), 50-65.

"When the Earth Moves." *National Geographic.* (May 1986), 638-39.

Wilford, John Noble. "Will We Ever Find Atlantis?" *New York Times,* November 11, 2003.

Williams, A. R. "After the Deluge." *National Geographic.* (November 1999), 108-129.

Raging Forces:

LIFE ON A VIOLENT PLANET

By George W. Stone

Published by the National Geographic Society
John M. Fahey, Jr., President and Chief Executive Officer
Gilbert M. Grosvenor, Chairman of the Board
Nina D. Hoffman, Executive Vice President;
    President, Book Publishing Group

Prepared by the Book Division
Kevin Mulroy, Senior Vice President and Publisher
Leah Bendavid-Val, Director of Photography Publishing
    and Illustrations
Marianne R. Koszorus, Director of Design

Barbara Brownell Grogan, Executive Editor
Elizabeth Newhouse, Director of Travel Publishing
Carl Mehler, Director of Maps

Staff for this book
Judith Klein, Project Editor
Diane Nelson, Art Director
Susan Blair, Illustrations Editor
Rob Waymouth, Illustrations Coordinator
Tracy Centorbi, Science Adviser
Rebecca Barnes, Susan Straight, Contributing Editors
Connie D. Binder, Indexer

Jennifer A. Thornton, Managing Editor
Gary Colbert, Production Director

Manufacturing and Quality Management
Christopher A. Liedel, Chief Financial Officer
Phillip L. Schlosser, Vice President
John T. Dunn, Technical Director
Chris Brown, Director
Maryclare Tracy, Manager
Nicole Elliott, Manager

Founded in 1888, the National Geographic Society is one of the largest nonprofit scientific and educational organizations in the world. It reaches more than 285 million people worldwide each month through its official journal, NATIONAL GEOGRAPHIC, and its four other magazines; the National Geographic Channel; television documentaries; radio programs; films; books; videos and DVDs; maps; and interactive media. National Geographic has funded more than 8,000 scientific research projects and supports an education program combating geographic illiteracy.

For more information, please call
1-800-NGS LINE (647-5463)
or write to the following address:

National Geographic Society
1145 17th Street N.W.
Washington, D.C. 20036-4688 U.S.A.

Visit us online at www.nationalgeographic.com

For information about special discounts
for bulk purchases, please contact
National Geographic Books Special Sales:
ngspecsales@ngs.org

Library of Congress Cataloging-in-Publication Data

Stone, George W.
    Raging forces : life on a violent planet / George W.
    Stone.
       p. cm.
    Includes index.
    ISBN 978-1-4262-0199-8 (regular)
    ISBN 978-0-7922-2965-0 (deluxe)
    1. Human ecology. 2. Human ecology—Religious
       aspects. 3. Nature—Effect of human beings on.
       4. Earth—Mythology. I. Title.
GF41.S765 2007
550—dc22   2007000518

Printed in the U.S.A.